LATIN AMERICA
BETWEEN THE
EAGLE AND THE BEAR

LATIN AMERICA
BETWEEN THE
EAGLE AND THE BEAR

by

SALVADOR DE MADARIAGA

LONDON

HOLLIS & CARTER

TO

THE MEMORY OF

ANITA EMMONS BLAINE

MADE AND PRINTED IN GREAT BRITAIN BY
CHARLES BIRCHALL & SONS LTD.,
LIVERPOOL AND LONDON, FOR
HOLLIS AND CARTER LIMITED,
25 ASHLEY PLACE, LONDON, S.W.1

CONTENTS

ACKNOWLEDGMENTS

M Y thanks are due to the Editor of the *Saturday Review* for having brought to my attention two valuable books: *The Struggle for Democracy in Latin America* by Charles G. Porter and Robert J. Alexander; and *Social Change in Latin America Today,* by various hands under the auspices of the Council on Foreign Relations; and to the publishers of the former for having put at my disposal a set of proofs of the work. I have profited by both books and often quoted from the second, for which I thank the authors and publishers. I have also to thank *The New Leader* for permission to quote from their pamphlet by Mr. Woytinsky, as specified in my footnotes. I have made ample use of the Chilean review *Estudios sobre el Comunismo* (Santiago de Chile) particularly in some sections of Chapter IV when dealing with the present state of communism in Latin America. I am also indebted to Professor Angel del Río for advice and data as to the relations between the two cultures in the American Continent; to Professor Perroux of the Collège de France for personal advice on economic relations as well as for his book *L'Europe sans Rivages,* to Mr. Leonard B. Schapiro for advice on Chapter IV, to Professor Falconelli, of Buenos Aires, for his paper on Chinese policy in Latin America; and to the Editor of the *China Quarterly* for his loan of the proofs of an article by Señor Victor Alba. I thank my assistant Mrs. Rauman for valuable advice in the preparation of the manuscript and my wife for her careful reading of the typescript.

INTRODUCTION

I N July and August 1960 I visited a number of countries in Latin America and was struck by the progress of pro-Soviet, perhaps rather anti-American, feeling wherever I went, particularly among students and professors as well as in the professional classes which, paradoxically enough, go by the name of liberal professions. It seemed to me that the world conjuncture was the very worst for such a situation to develop on the very doorstep of the United States; for we are witnessing a regular outburst of political liberty and national independence in two other continents in circumstances which by no stretch of imagination can be said to contribute to a stable order, and the world can ill afford to set a third continent in turmoil.

We are everywhere seeing the forms of liberal democracy jeopardized; twisted and tortured by foreign oppression in communist-dominated countries, as in Eastern Europe, or by a home-grown form of oppression, as in Yugoslavia or in Spain; and exposed to the hazards of inexperience and of a more vigorous than intelligent nationalism, as in a number of newborn Asian and African "nations". *Nations*. As if, on the one hand, this typically European and relatively modern concept were applicable to the Asian and African *peoples* on which it is being inflicted by a Europeanized Americanized anti-European anti-American *élite;* and as if the concept was not already on its way out even in Europe and in America. Disorder and confusion are the inevitable dust-clouds in the wake of such agitated events. Now, disorder and confusion are as favourable to communism as they are injurious to liberal democracy.

The affairs of men are ruled by a kind of law of sociological gravity which forces them to fall towards chaos if not held at a certain level of order by an intelligent hand. This intelligent hand is what we call *government*. It is plain that in a number of cases too great for the peace of mind of the world, the hand that keeps the affairs of men from falling into chaos is neither strong nor intelligent enough to fulfil its task. It follows that in wide areas of the world circumstances are being created which favour communism, since communism thrives in disorder and confusion while liberal democracy requires calm and the rule of law.

Such being the general picture, we must look on the considerable progress made by communism in Latin America as a serious threat to our civilization, particularly as this progress is observable mostly among the intellectual classes. In the United States, one gathers the impression that the intellectual is an oddity, a freak, at times a joke. His opinions are heard with polite deference and soon forgotten. As for his chances of a political career, they simply do not exist. A flavour of intellectuality has barred access to the White House to Mr Adlai Stevenson, and one wonders whether Mr Kennedy's success may not be due to the cleverness with which he hid his intellectuality (I am not saying "his intelligence") from his suspicious voters. The situation may be evolving. To be a Harvard professor is no longer a disqualification for becoming a member of the Presidential Cabinet; but to have published a book of poems might still be so.

Now in Latin America a man may be writing poetry on Friday and become President or Minister of Foreign Affairs the following Sunday. The why and the how of this will have to be elucidated further on, and it is a fascinating story; but for the present we need do no more than note the fact. Nor should the observation be limited to that form of power which derives from actual political functions. It cannot be doubted, for instance, that the high reputation which Pablo Neruda enjoys as a poet considerably enhances his power over Chilean public opinion as a communist leader.

No more grievous mistake could therefore be made by the

public opinion of the United States than to shrug its shoulders at the pro-Soviet and anti-American wave which is sweeping the intellectual circles of Latin America. From the ranks of these pink professors, poets, doctors and lawyers, the men will be recruited who will actually govern Latin America not merely ten years hence, but may be next year, or maybe next month. The issue is immediate and urgent; and we must waste no time in facing it.

In the pages that follow I have tried to present in succession the four orders of questions that the problem raises, or, perhaps better, the four aspects that the problem presents, namely: Latin American, Spanish, American and Soviet. The first seems to me of the utmost importance. While responsible Latin Americans realize how local and national for the most part the causes of their troubles are, one is apt to find among less mature minds a tendency to shift the burden of responsibility on to the United States. This attitude is only too easy: it has the twofold advantage of unloading the heart from its burden of frustration and of relieving the brain from its duty to enquire. It is unfortunately widespread from Mexico to Patagonia. And yet, if the third aspect—that of the actual responsibility of the United States—is to be adequately understood, a clear and objective statement of the responsibility of the Latin American nations themselves must be first recorded. For it would be an insult to them to come to the conclusion that they have no share—indeed that theirs is not the main share—in the shaping of the condition they are in.

The Spanish aspect must also be analysed, the more so as it is nearly always minimized to vanishing point by most American writers on these subjects. Without an adequate realization of this aspect, the situation cannot be understood and therefore cannot be adequately met. Strange as this may seem to some observers, who too readily assume that all would be well if only Latin America went the way of Texas and New Mexico, the Spanishness of Latin America is, as I hope to show, an essential ingredient for the future of the continent.

A survey of the American aspect needs no justification. Every now and then we are treated to a picturesque pious platitude about non-intervention, not merely by politicians, for whom it may be a necessary evil, but by university professors and such other free lances, in whose case the evil would not appear to be necessary at all. The fact is that the predominance of the United States in the New World is overwhelming, and her responsibility accordingly high. A study of American policy and of its critics, including a criticism of such critics, must therefore be at least sketched.

Finally there is the Soviet aspect, the importance of which requires no special emphasis. For the Soviet Union, a national conversion to communism in the American continent is bound to assume an even greater importance than such a conversion in any other continent (save perhaps Europe). Latin America lies so far away from Russia that no accusation of military action could be levelled against the Soviet Union as was done with only too much justification in Eastern European cases.* Here communism would conquer unaided and by virtue of its own powers of conviction. This is, more or less, the case of Cuba. Another such victory—and they have been round the corner in Chile and in Venezuela—and a wave of fashion, imitation and infatuation for communism might sweep the whole continent.

---

*Considerable Soviet military help has been shipped to Cuba after Castro's victory over Batista, but the struggle which brought him to power was backed by western arms.

I

THE LATIN AMERICAN ASPECT

I.—GENERAL ATTITUDE

THERE is no denying that Latin America suffers from a certain sense of frustration. It feels neglected, forgotten, far away from the centres where history is made. Once an important, an almost predominant part of an impressive world empire, it is now but a motley crowd of nations with little or no international weight. Few of her men of science reach world renown; few of her men of letters are read; few of her statesmen attain a reputation other than that which courtesy or convenience suggests. The Latin American nations, in short, feel that they are rather objects than subjects of history. Things happen to them or are done to them. They do not generate at home.

And yet, for the most part the cause of this weakness of the nations of Latin America is autochtonous. The very place and shape of the earth it occupies accounts for much of its difficulties. It is placed on the confines of the world, on the edge of the solitary, immense Pacific, and facing the immense and solitary Antarctic; and its several nations are dispersed in a wide arc around Brazil up and down the forbidding fastness of the Andes, or, beyond the impassable forests of the Isthmus, on the high plains of Mexico. Nature has laid out Latin America in striking contrast with either Europe or the United States, whose very shapes lend themselves far better to a round-the-hearth sort of life, gathering together the nations or States that compose the group in amicable converse.

This circumstance (which air-navigation is gradually modifying and possibly conquering) has increased the sense of isolation and neglect which can be observed in a number of Latin

American nations. The ardent nationalism of some of them often springs from this isolation as a compensating effect. It is often less the direct outcome of pride in achievement (comparable, say, to British nationalism) than a derivate or secondary feeling; a come-back of the feeling of being oppressed by frustration which expands in proud nationalism to recover its full size.

Feeling is therefore bound to enter into the composition of Latin American public opinion perhaps in a higher degree than is the case elsewhere. A feeling of hurt pride and of injustice undergone. If such emotions tend to be polarized against the United States, this is obviously due to the fact that the United States has become the omnipresent, omniactive nation in the continent. From this point of view it matters little that the concrete action considered be "good" or "bad", well or ill inspired. The trouble lies deeper than the categories of "good" and "evil". It is historical, human, cosmic. A score of weak nations, poor in the midst of their natural riches, scattered over huge territories, heirs to a powerful and colourful past, but divided by nature and character, struggling to raise themselves to the status they think theirs by natural right, look with impatience, and at times with resentment, on the power, wealth and success of a *parvenu* nation which was still uncouth and rustic when they were already highly civilized.

This point must be stressed, awkward as it may be in some ways, because it is essential. The Socratic-Christian tradition of European civilization is older and stronger in Hispano- than it is in Anglo-America. Furthermore, (for reasons which will be examined later in Chapter 2) the Hispanic cultural milieu tends to produce types of mankind more sensitive to the elusive and subtle values than does the empirical and positive Anglo-Saxon. It follows that not infrequently the powerful, successful man of the North is placed by tyrannous circumstances in a position to order about and humiliate a man who, much as he respects the Northerner's know-how, is prone to feel disdainful about his humanistic horizons; and this kind of situation, repeated to the thousand, ends by determining the emotional environment in a mood hostile to the North.

The recent trend towards seeing in the United States the Mecca which France had become after the wars of independence had ousted Spain from that position should not be overestimated. It acts, of course, in compensation to balance the anti-American feeling aroused for the reasons suggested above as well as for other reasons that will turn up in due time. There is in Latin America a genuine admiration for the technical achievements of the North. While twenty or forty years ago a wealthy patient would go to Paris for a major operation he is nowadays more likely to go to New York; while older generations would send their sons to the Sorbonne or to the Parisian technical schools, they would rather send them now to Harvard or the MIT. Nor is at any rate the well-informed man averse to appreciating the good will, friendliness and kindness of the average American. Life is too complex not to admit and fuse all these emotional contradictions. All in all, however, the resulting attitude is adverse. So that the movements of public opinion as determined by the tides and waves of political events operate on a raw material which far from being neutral and passive is polarized in an antagonistic direction towards the United States.

2. — RICH AND POOR

This attitude, consciously or not, tends to identify the United States with wealth. It so happens, however, that Latin America is a country in which the rich are very rich and the poor very poor. The reasons vary but the outcome is ever the same. In some countries, such as Argentina, poverty is rather the outcome of the political mismanagement of vast natural resources, coupled with an unfortunate demographic trend towards concentrating in vast urban agglomerations; in short, a process of liberal-capitalistic accumulation of wealth gone awry through mishandling. In other countries, such as Peru, Ecuador, Bolivia, the causes of the disparity in wealth levels include the reluctance of the native population to adopt European ways. In the first case, it means living in slum-like conditions and wasting anything between two and four hours a day in uncomfortable, unreliable and tedious transportation. In the second, it means realizing what European life is like without being able or even feeling capable of rising to it unaided. A more detailed description of the variety of forms which this contrast between rich and poor takes in the several countries of Latin America would add colour to the general picture but might possibly blur its design, which is what matters. The chief point to record here is that in all Latin America (with the exception of Uruguay and Costa Rica) the contrast between rich and poor is too stark for political health.

Taken as a whole, Latin America is by no means a depressed area of the world. Its average income per head was $240 in 1950, comparable therefore to that of Italy; though it varied from $480 dollars for Venezuela to $90 for Bolivia, Nicaragua and Paraguay. But in the case of Peru, for instance, the million inhabitants of Lima enjoyed an income of $445 per head as against an average of $50 left for the other seven and a half million; and one could not move among the Limanians for a week without realizing that the average of $445 was overtopped many times by the wealthy and never as much as dreamt of by the poor inhabitants of that showy city.

In conclusion, the daily confrontation of wealth and misery is starker perhaps in Latin America than in any other land; and, therefore, the psychological situation thus created is apt to foster a resentment propitious to communist movements and to attract to communism men and women with stronger hearts than brains.

3. — CHARACTER OF THE MIDDLE CLASS

It is often said that Latin America suffers from the lack of a middle class. This is not so. One would be rather tempted to say that the very reverse is the truth, for in a certain, concrete sort of way, it is rather from an excess than from a lack of a middle class that Latin American countries suffer.

The two views, however, can be reconciled when we come to closer grips with the subject. There is too much of the idle, unproductive or merely administrative kind of middle class; not enough, and to a disastrous degree, of the truly productive and creative kind.

The average young man feels drawn to an intellectual occupation. The best will reach independent positions, enabling the lucky possessor of a talent in sufficient demand to be self-employed. The less fortunate will seek situations mostly in the giving of the government, including university chairs, the civil service, the armed forces and so forth. Journalism and other professions (such as municipal civil services) will absorb the rest. But there is a tendency towards a permanent white-collar unemployment everywhere, and a consequent dilution of services and of salaries.

Technical and scientific careers are neglected. This fact (the origin of which will be discussed in the second chapter) explains in part the dependence of Latin America on foreign capital; for lacking an adequate supply of reliable local technicians local capital will hesitate to take risks. It also explains the political weakness of the middle classes in Latin America, in what concerns the discharge of their chief sociological function: the defining and upholding of standards of public and collective behaviour and objective criticism of the government.

This situation tends to worsen the effects of the contrast between rich and poor noted above; for though numerically big enough, the middle class is too weak and too poor to soften the transition as it does, for instance, in England or in France, or even in Italy. Furthermore, owing to its modest and precarious standard of living this dependent middle class is more apt to feel drawn to communism; the more so as, by its very nature, it lacks experience of working-class and industrial conditions, and is prone to consider things from an intellectualistic and abstract angle.

4.—UNIVERSITY TRENDS

Up to a point, the shortcomings of the middle class are closely related to those of the university. In spite of an undoubted wealth in individual talents, the universities of Latin America leave much to be desired. Their chief failures, from our present point of view, would appear to be due to a certain laxity in organization and rules amounting in some extreme cases to sheer demagogy and even anarchy.

A few concrete examples will illustrate these points. In the Law Faculty of the University of Buenos Aires twenty thousand students are on the registers. Of these, no more than about eight thousand are considered genuine; the remaining twelve thousand are hangers-on who find it in their interest to retain their student status for a variety of reasons, including in a fairly high number of cases in order to recruit and organize communist contingents.

There would appear to be no rule (or no desire to apply it if such a rule exists) to eliminate from the precincts of the university men and women who are not genuine students. In particular those who have failed in their examinations seem to be allowed to try and try again for ever. To the best of my information, a "student" may fail time and again and still remain a student for as long as he wishes, not only wasting the time of his teachers and the space of his classes, but acquiring the long experience of university-life which will enable him to boss its political activity.

In the University of Trujillo, north of Lima, I was told that at the time I was there (end of August 1960) there were forty students in training under Castro's guerrilla instructors in Cuba; they were due to remain three months. Another group of forty students was held in readiness to replace them on their return. I enquired whether it was possible for a student of the university to vanish for three months and be admitted on his return as if nothing had happened, and the answer was "Yes".

I might quote even worse cases of indiscipline, indeed of anarchy, in Latin American universities were they relevant to our present purpose. But what is relevant is that, in most cases, the professorial staff is not adequately remunerated. This puts a premium on any allurement that Peking or Moscow may offer, not, of course, in a direct attempt at purchasing consciences, which in nearly every case would fail, but in such things as invitations to visit those far-off, alluring and picturesque countries. The cases I have known seem to have been rewarding to the far-away hosts. Though not precisely converted to communism the rectors and professors do come back impressed and ready to praise.

5. — POLITICAL INSTABILITY

The political instability of Latin America is now proverbial. It has in no small measure contributed to lowering her reputation in the rest of the world; in its turn, it has been judged perhaps too harshly because of a general prejudice and predisposition to look down on Latin American things, on which more will have to be said later.

This attitude is the more unfair to the Latin American nations for the fact that their instability has been more often than not inflicted on them. And they are aware of it. Here is what a distinguished Uruguayan essayist has to say on this delicate matter:

> Is it not proved that most of the "revolutions", frequent in this America, have been secretly promoted, financed and made use of by agents of foreign capitalism? Is it not equally proved that as many of these "revolutions" had no other aim than to seize hold of the government in order to be able to negotiate from there with the big financial trusts which enabled illustrious statesmen to amass fat fortunes on the basis of the enslavement of the nation? Is it not a fact that the Chaco war, which bled Bolivia and Paraguay white for over two years, was secretly ruled by the rival interests of foreign oil companies?*

*"La Tragedia del Indio" by Alberto Zum Felde, in *Cuadernos Americanos*, 1943.

Leaving aside these unhealthy extraneous causes, the political instability of the Latin American nations may be explained by local conditions. The natural setting of most of the Latin American nations does not favour a calm and uneventful national life. It is either too mountainous and broken, as in Peru, or too vast though flat, as in Argentina, and nearly always too large for the population which inhabits it. In such geographic and demographic circumstances, the obstacles in the way of political institutions are almost insuperable. Roads and railways, for instance, are the very veins and arteries of the body politic. How is a nation to build them in an adequate measure and to keep them working when a man can travel for hundreds of miles without sighting a human being, or when nearly impassable peaks, abysses or deserts separate one valley from the next? When most Latin American nations cover areas twice or three times as wide as that of an average European nation, and are inhabited by anything between a third and a tenth of the population one expects in an average European nation, how can we demand of them the order and stability of Europe?

Furthermore, at the close of the wars of emancipation these nations found themselves in a kind of political no man's land. They were the heirs of a political tradition which they had to reject; and the enthusiastic followers of a new set of political values which they perhaps naïvely dreamt of transplanting root, stem and foliage to their own lands. France was to be the model for their political philosophy; the United States, the model for their constitutions.

We can hardly blame them for having made in 1830 the mistake the whole world is making in 1960. Political institutions cannot be transplanted. I know of no sight more pathetic than that of an African "Speaker" sweating under an English wig in the tropical heat of an African "House of Commons". When the Latin American countries imported such formulas as "Liberty-Equality-Fraternity" to the continent of the three colours and a rainbow of cultures, when they brought universal suffrage to countries suffering from a sparse population and a lack of roads, let alone illiteracy and un-European ways of life, what could be expected but a century of strife?

Again, the deeper nature of this strife, which is psychological, can only be adequately dealt with in our second chapter. Here it is only mentioned as one of the circumstances which is contributing to the spread of communism. The fact is that Latin America has not yet found a political system close-fitting enough to her way of being to lead a stable life. And since no such system has proved itself good enough, why not try communism? This is the shape things take under this angle.

6. — GENERALS AND DOCTORS

Hence the importance of these two typically Latin American forces in political life: the army and the dictatorship. We have here to return to what was said above about political strife throughout the nineteenth century. The French and American models met with the resistance opposed to them by the way of being of the peoples who were being asked to adopt them. Who asked? Who resisted?

Those who asked were the "doctors". Those who resisted were the "generals". They are the two prototypes of Latin American public life. The doctor will be nearly always a lawyer, with intellectual interests far wider than mere law, and whose reading will reach out to Baudelaire at least as willingly as to Grotius. He may or may not have studied at the Sorbonne (if over forty), at Harvard (if younger); but his culture will be by no means shallow. He will dream of his country as a well-regulated Switzerland (if his country is small) or as a powerful and respected United States (if his country is big). He wants a parliamentary system, *á la française,* or a presidential system, the American way, but he feels true abhorrence for those *pronunciamientos* and military régimes which, in his eyes, rob his country of prestige in the world of nations. His chief passion is personal and national respectability. More often than not he will be a dweller in the national capital, will write articles, books, poems perhaps, but will possess but little knowledge of the way of life at the other end of the nation, where simpler men, white, Indian or mixed, struggle with the earth, the weather, animals and local bosses. His trend will be towards principles and general (if not abstract) views.

The general is not interested in principles at all. He is, in the American phrase, a go-getter. His aim is power, and he feels no qualms as to the means and ways to attain it, nor indeed to retain it. He may be an officer with a certain level of technical military training and education, but, not infrequently, will be a self-made general, having reached the top of the military ladder by unorthodox ways, and a self-taught man, more self than taught. His knowledge of the roots of the country, the village square, pond, drink shop and police station, will be concrete and extensive. He will often be of mixed blood in countries rich in Indian stock. He will be astute, ruthless and, if need be, cruel. He will sometimes overlay his power lust with ideals, and not always insincerely, but in that case his ideals will seldom if ever rise beyond nationalism, and will not stray towards either respect for the individual or deference to world public opinion; nor would they ever stand in the way of his own personal ambition. He will evince an insatiable thirst for wealth, a deep suspicion of independent thought, a watchful jealousy of possible rivals and a quick readiness to sell his services abroad if he can thereby gain prestige and power for himself and his régime.

The doctor and the general are the oil and the vinegar of all Latin American political salads. What one is likely to find in actual life are mixtures in all proportions of these two undiluted ingredients. At times one finds a "doctor" under a general's uniform (General Aramburu, for instance); at times, a "general" lurks behind the plain clothes of a doctor (Dr Laureano Gómez, for instance). In most cases, Latin American countries oscillate between generalized doctors and doctorized generals, or, in shorter terms, between left and right. If the doctor lacks some of the general's qualities (energy, astuteness, knowledge of the roots of the country), he will be ousted by a general who, unhindered by any of the doctor's qualms, will then settle in power as a dictator.

7.—IMITATION OF THE UNITED STATES

This pendulum-like form of instability which afflicts Latin America is fostered by an unfortunate tendency to imitate American institutions and policies whether they are commendable in themselves or not, and whether, if commendable for the United States, they are adaptable to the circumstances of Latin America.

The most obvious case is the presidential system and the election of the President by a direct massive vote of the population. It would be a waste of time and space to discuss here whether the American way of electing a President is good or bad for the United States. It is enough to show that it is disastrous for the Latin American countries (most of them) which have (more or less faithfully) imitated it. Even in the United States it is bound to lead to a certain amount of demagogy; in Latin America it sinks hopelessly into it. One of the chief causes of political instability in Latin America is therefore this sorry imitation of the United States in constitutional matters; and, as instability and the mass-vote are both factors favouring a stampede towards communism, it follows that, paradoxically enough, it is by imitating the United States that Latin America is risking a communist infection.

This imitation is at times harmless enough. *Casa Rosada*, the name given in Buenos Aires to the residence of the President, is but an obvious pastiche of the White House. But when it comes to imitating the Gargantuan appetite for paper evinced by American immigration authorities, matters become more serious, not without at times turning comic. Two Latin American nations a few years ago thought it no doubt up to date to imitate the United States by taking the finger prints of all persons applying for a visa. When the United States realized that such a measure was odious to the edge of silliness and withdrew it, the two Latin American imitators found themselves in the dilemma of either remaining as sole witnesses to an obsolete past or following sheepishly in the steps of their model.

But the paper and rubber stamp curtain which the United

States has erected round herself to guard against visitors is still generally imitated in Latin America. Why? God only knows (though I may venture to reveal some of His secrets in my next chapter), for there is no apparent reason why the Spanish- and Portuguese-speaking nations of this continent should erect such paper barriers, even if there are reasons for so doing in the case of the United States (which I frankly do not know). The ingenuity of the Latin American nations for inventing printed forms of all kinds meant to circumvent the evil intentions of the well-meaning visitor (as for the evil-meaning one, nothing can stop him) would humiliate the most skilful form-designer and rule-drafter of the Department of Immigration of the United States.

And there is pride in it too. A distinguished Latin American who happened at the time to live in exile, related to me how, visiting the Mexican Consul for a visa, and being asked if his papers were in order, he was tactless enough to answer: "Of course. I have just got my visa at the American Consulate." The Mexican official grew stiff: "That means nothing. We are just as difficult as they are."

Indeed, like the Americans, the Mexicans are not content with stamping a visa on a page of your passport; they must give you a separate paper of their own to clip to your passport and fatten it; and when you pass the frontier, you must sign and have signed all kinds of forms which when accumulated in the central services in their thousands and their millions must rejoice the heart of every bureaucrat worth his ink.

8.—IMMIGRATION

This mania for paper-barriers in imitation of the United States is in its turn inspired by an even less justified imitation of the same model. The United States may not too unreasonably have come to the conclusion that she must restrict the influx of immigrants seeking to settle on her territory. The nations of Latin America can put forward no such argument. Though their birth rate (about 2.5 per cent yearly) is one of the highest, if not the highest, in the world, they are still underpopulated to a degree that precludes an adequate political organization. This may be one of the reasons for the *weakness of being* from which they suffer. May I explain? Nations differ in the amount or strength of being they are endowed with. Britain and Switzerland possess more being than Germany or Spain; by which I mean that Britain is more Britain and Switzerland is more Switzerland than Germany is Germany or Spain is Spain. I believe that though rich in being the United States has less of it than Britain. It is not power, it is the amount of force wherewith you are what you are.

This applies to nations, not to peoples. Most Latin American peoples are rich in being, indeed in many ways they might be said to be richer in being than the Anglo-Americans; as every Anglo-American who has visited Mexico, Peru, Guatemala or Chile knows. The weakness here described refers to the organized, conscious form or vessel of a people, the "nervous", "arterial" and "muscular" collective systems which enable it to react with a greater or lesser consistency and unity to outside influences or dangers.

The Latin American nations are in this sense poor in being, even though they may be rich in being as peoples. Mexico, perhaps the least poor of them, is still far less rich in being than her more nationalistic sons believe. And the main reason for this is the same for all of them. They are too vast for their population and so, as the striking Spanish phrase goes, "their souls wander about in their bodies".

They are loosely woven nations less like cloth than like network tissue, not merely in space but in time; they possess but little consistency, both because at any time their texture is not strong enough to withstand the impact of the moment, but also because this texture is apt to change from one moment to the next.

This is due in part to the fact that the nations of Latin America happen to be composed of either shallow layers of a white upper and middle class on an Indian basis, or else a slack network of European civilization stretched to tearing point and beyond so as to clothe, without altogether covering, vast empty spaces. There are of course all kinds of intermediate stages. Mexico, for instance, is rich in white and less than white layers over her Indian basis, and Uruguay has less space to offer than Argentina; but the thinness of the European *élite* and the vastness of the nearly empty space are the two "polar" features that apply in a greater or lesser degree to all Latin American countries. Between the huge central cities and the far-off pueblos and small farms scattered over field and mountain there lives hardly any spot of collective activity, social tissue, knot or institution capable of ensuring enough organic continuity for the adequate working of the whole. The primary evil, there-fore, is lack of population.

But the *beati possidentes* of the nations such as they now are do not think so. And in imitation of the United States, they close the door to immigrants, indeed some of them even more strictly so. Those who do not, Venezuela, for instance, flourish accord-ingly, and enjoy the highest average income per head in Latin America. The worst case may well be that of Mexico where a strong prejudice against immigration struggles against reason and commonsense to rationalize itself as an attitude in defence of the Indian; while both reflection and experience show that what the Indian needs is an influx of enterprising Europeans, preferably Spaniards or Italians, who create new productive units and rapidly raise him up the economic ladder. In this sense, the strong injection of Spanish blood received by Mexico as the outcome of the Spanish civil war and the outburst of creative activity which it generated, is a lesson which blind prejudice refuses to admit. More on this will have to be said anon. Mean-while the income per head of the population of Mexico (despite her remarkable progress in recent years) stands at $115, com-pared to Venezuela's $480 and Uruguay's $395.

9. — LAND MONOPOLIES

One of the almost inevitable consequences of this state of affairs has been the development of huge land monopolies for which the word *latifundia* is insufficient, since they are so vast that they would deserve the name of *macrofundia,* were such a hybrid permitted. These huge land estates are often attributed to the viceregal period. True enough, in the Spanish days, magnates and others standing well at Court were able to obtain estates the magnitude of which was unsuspected by the naïve official in Madrid who granted so many miles in width from the coast to the Cordillera crest. But the origin of modern macrofundia is in most cases far more recent, and due to a misguided nineteenth-century "liberalism". Here is (as concerns Mexico) the opinion of a Mexican expert:

> The situation of a considerable part of the native Mexican population became worse as the outcome of the effect on communal land ownership (deeply rooted in pre-hispanic days) of the law of July 25th, 1856, which in its essence aimed at disentailing the lands of Church communities. This abolition of communal ownership brought about the result that most natives either were dispossessed of every legal right to their ownership of their lands or else when receiving individual ownership titles, sold them for a trifle. This explains for a good part the development of latifundia during President Porfirio Diaz's regime and the consequent impoverishment of the native peasantry who went to swell the ranks of the indigent social class of the "Peons" or life-workers in the landed estates.*

So much for Mexico. Similar conclusions, though from a variety of premisses, may be drawn with regard to other countries. In Colombia, for instance, there were during the nineteenth century several streams of gifts of government lands (old Spanish Crown lands) to several generations of persons to whom the nation was supposed to be grateful, let alone the selling away of Church lands as in Mexico; the first turned into latifundia lands which should be useful today for colonization by immigrants; the second did many an Indian community out of

*Dr Miguel Leon Portilla, director of the Instituto Indigenista Interamericano, in *Combate,* No. 13, Mexico, Nov.-Dec. 1960.

its best, i.e., its communal lands. These Indian communities were creations of the agrarian policy of the Spanish Crown and they combined collective with private ownership in the old Castilian way, which by the way was similarly destroyed in Spain by similar "liberal", anti-clerical measures in the nineteenth century.

Quite apart from these origins of latifundia, there are causes due to modern capitalistic pressure. It is certain that a well-known *macrofundium* owned by a German in northern Peru owes little of its 75 Km by 500 Km acreage to the Spanish viceroys, and much to the skilful use of finance and water-rights; and that similarly vast *macrofundia* owned by British and American meat-packing firms in Argentina were unknown to San Martín.

The sober fact is that such sociological phenomena nearly always spring from a knot of objective circumstances, such as conditions favourable for extensive rather than intensive cultivation, lack of native capital, or of skill or interest in land cultivation on the part of too many nationals, illiteracy and poverty in the peasantry, and defective legislation. In their turn, these huge land monopolies tend to stabilize or even foster the ills of the body politic from which they spring; from our point of view, in particular, they must be considered as a danger in that by divorcing too many persons from private ownership they enlarge the dispossessed class in which communism can always hope to find converts.

10.—MINING AND INDUSTRY

Similar observations could be made on mining and industry. There is considerable mineral wealth in Latin America; but its extraction, elaboration and exploitation are predominantly in the hands of foreign firms. The chief reasons for this are three: political disorder during the nineteenth century when its inevitable counterpart, financial chaos, led to much giving away of national wealth;* lack of home capital, a lack either genuine or

*This began with the wars of liberation when Bolívar and Santander gave away national mineral wealth to pay for war expenses or for loans.

brought about by the export of national capital by its owners both for business and for pleasure; lack of technicians.

These three circumstances might have been disastrous for Latin America; they were less than disastrous, though bad enough. They gave rise to at least two serious evils; in the days of unscrupulous capitalism, they tended to impoverish the Latin American countries by foreign-owned enterprises rich in tricks. By watering capital, charging heavy prices for goods (loco-motives, for instance, for foreign-owned railways) and such other devices, the foreign companies extorted benefits much higher than met the eye out of the service rendered. The service, nevertheless, was there and though too expensive was an actual service for all that. The second evil was the grafting of foreign concerns into the body politic of the nation, amounting to States within the State, a fact which, though in many concrete ways favourable to the local communities and even to the whole nation concerned, aroused dangerous psychological tensions both on the individual and the national plane; particularly as such big concerns were often able to influence and, at times, to control the political life of the host country.

From our point of view, this state of affairs gave rise to fields of activity and growth for communism, since it developed popu-lous zones of workers often an easy prey to campaigns of resent-ment based on class war and on nationalism.

II. — WORKING-CLASS MONOPOLIES

The weakness of the nation's "being" and the slackness of the State have originated in a number of Latin American nations a curious development of working-class unions (*sindicatos*) strong enough to become in a way States within the State. Latin American Unions differ from the type of working-class organizations prevalent in Europe. Nor are they by any means alike from one country to another. It is a far cry from on the one hand the Argentine Unions, fermenting in an air hot with political passions, struggling between Socialist, Catholic, Com-munist and Peronist tendencies and leaders, and on the other the

Mexican Unions shunning the mere political game in order to cultivate positive power in the shade of that curious and original presidential system within which few things are what they profess to be, few cogwheels actually turn around their own axles, and yet all manage to gear in (outwardly at any rate) perfect order.

One thing is certain. In most Latin American countries, the working-class Unions are powerful enough to challenge the State; and in some, notably Argentina and Mexico, they may well be too powerful for the nation's health.* That in certain conditions in certain Latin American countries this weakness of the State towards the Unions might lead to a communist putsch can by no means be excluded.

12. — THE CHURCH

It goes without saying that the Church for Latin America means the Catholic Church. By and large, Latin America is Catholic. She is much less devout, indeed much less aware of what being Catholic actually means, than she is Catholic as a matter of course. A man (most men, very likely) will be baptized, married and buried under the rites of the Church while hardly ever going to church for anything else; and yet he will consider himself a Catholic. The Catholic religion in Latin America is therefore less a faith or a moral discipline than a kind of air one breathes.

This, however, does not go for the Indians or the mestizos with a strong ratio of native blood. In their case, religion has become and remains a deeply felt emotion the exact nature of which is unfathomable to us. It is a part of their life. The devout men and women who, in penitence or hope, slowly progress on their knees along the long way that leads them to the altar of Our Lady of Guadalupe on the outskirts of Mexico City, the

*As an instance of this excessive power wielded without restraint or respect, the Spanish-language monthly, *Cuadernos,* edited in Paris by the Congress for Freedom of Culture, cannot be sold in Mexico City's stands because the Union of Newspaper Street Vendors, under communist control, vetoes it.

old woman who relates, argues, expostulates, begs and explains her troubles to the Virgin in a sombre aisle of Puebla cathedral, live in a world of religion which interpenetrates and deepens their daily world.

What does this complex situation which religion occupies in Latin American life signify for the social and political role of the Church? Under the Jacobin influences which drove the leftish "doctors" of Latin America during the nineteenth century, the Church has gradually lost the strong official position it had enjoyed during the three centuries of Spanish rule. Definite measures for separating it from the State have been adopted by eleven countries, and in the others such as Argentina, union does not always work to its advantage.

The most formidable Church as a political and sociological force may well be that of Colombia. In the old days it actually chose the candidate who was to be elected President; and it is said that the long conservative monopoly of the presidency ceased because Archbishop Perdomo in a moment of vacillation gave his blessing to two candidates and thus split the vote. The Colombian Church controls education to an extent perhaps unknown anywhere in the world outside Spain. The most firmly secularized of the Latin American nations is perhaps Mexico, where the Church has even undergone a period of fierce persecution amounting at times to civil war. Shortly after leaving office, though not power, in 1931, President Calles said to me, not without feeling: "The best thing that could happen to this country would be that a dynamite bomb were exploded under the church of Guadalupe." And yet, I am assured that among the many almost contradictory conditions a Mexican presidential candidate must fulfil to succeed must be that he is acceptable to the Church.

It is, of course, a fact that the Catholic Church, though far less powerful than in olden times, indeed perhaps less and less powerful as times go by, is still a political and sociological force in Latin America. How used, and in what direction is another matter. Its record could have been better at the origin of dictatorships, but it could have been worse at the end of some of them;

for though it was not without some ambiguous responsibility in the access of Perón, it actually contributed not a little to his downfall as well as to that of other deposed tyrants such as Pérez Jiménez (Venezuela), Rojas Pinilla (Colombia) and Batista (Cuba); nor is it altogether passive in the struggle against Stroessner (Paraguay) and Trujillo (Dominican Republic). Christian democratic parties exist in a number of countries, following a line possibly more conservative than that of their European counterparts.

From our point of view, however, that of the communist threat to Latin America, a *caveat* must be entered, to guard against the all too easy argument that a predominantly Catholic atmosphere is a bar to communism. This view is not merely far from the truth: it is the very reverse of the truth. Unfortunate though it happens to be, a Catholic milieu can be favourable to the growth of communism. This much could be said on the strength of what goes on in Europe, where France and Italy, two Catholic countries, are burdened with the two most powerful communist parties in the whole free world.

The reason for this may well turn out to be twofold. The first is the authoritarian nature of the Catholic Church and dogma, which in shape and style, though not in content, is similar enough to communism to suggest a conscious imitation of Rome by Moscow. When in the early 'thirties a young Spanish friend of mine went to Moscow to study communism on the spot with a letter of introduction I gave him for Litvinov, he returned with the news that one of Lenin's favourite authors was St Ignatius Loyola. If it is not true, then it deserves to be true. For there are a number of features in the Company of Jesus which apply to communism as to the manner born.

One cannot glance at communist debates and polemical disputes without perceiving a flavour similar to that of the scholastic disputations of old: the same reliance on texts quoted from Marx or Lenin as in the old days from St Augustine or St Thomas; the same dropping of texts when they became heretical (Stalin); the same frowning at deviations (heresies); the same inquisition and the same stakes. Though the Catholic Church has shed the old slough of intransigence which disfigured it, it remains dogmatic and certain of its truth. Insofar as it shapes minds and hearts in the direction of certainty and rejection of deviationists, it may be said to constitute a kind of preparatory training for the development of the communist sort of mind. Disenchanted communists often turn Catholic.

<h2 style="text-align:center">13. — RADICALISM</h2>

It goes without saying that no amount of Catholic dogmatism and intellectual discipline can lead a faithful son of the Church to communism. The faith is the guarantee that such a disaster cannot happen, for while the lamp of the faith still illumines the spirit of the faithful, spiritual values are safe and materialism can be kept at bay.

But what happens when the lamp goes out? It is here that a Catholic country runs the risk of slipping into communism. The totalitarian tendency inherent in the Catholic Church leads it to claim as much political power as the nation concerned will allow. A glance at what happens in Spain, where, for reasons of his own, the dictator has given a free run to the totalitarian appetite of the Church, suffices to show that in such cases the whole spiritual and cultural life of the citizen falls, whether he likes it or not, under the sway of the Church.

This explains how it is only in Catholic countries that anti-clerical parties are strong. They spring from the meeting of two currents: one negative, self-defence against an all-invading Church; another positive, the Jacobin philosophy which flourishes in the French eighteenth century and fructifies in the French Revolution feeding the whole nineteenth with its dry but nutritious fruit.

Now, what distinguishes this radicalism, as it came to be known, is that while anti-Catholic in substance it managed nevertheless to retain some Catholic features in trend and style. It was, and is, prone to dogmatism. Do not expect of it the empirical latitudinarian aloofness of English liberalism. The radical knows what truth is no less definitely than does the

Catholic; for the simple reason that he is a Catholic the wrong way round. Nothing is more like +8 than −8.

This explains why, in our dangerous days in Latin America, there are more communists and sympathizers to be found among intellectuals and middle-class professionals than among manual workers. They are radicals; men conscious of what is intellectually at stake; shaped for dogmatism by either the Catholic Church or the anti-Catholic university, in both cases, trained in dogmatism. From them, rather than from the simple, uneducated and empirical working classes, the menace comes which might lock up freedom in a fortress guarded by Soviet tanks.

14.—DICTATORSHIPS

There is a chain of thought which runs: "We are democrats; *ergo* we are anti-dictators; the United States favours dictators, therefore we are anti-Americans; the Russians are anti-American; therefore we are pro-Russians; the Russians are communists, therefore we are pro-communist." Rather than a chain of thought, this is of course a chain of nonsense, which shows that it really is a chain of emotion. It will have to be examined more closely further on.

For the present, our concern is with the relation of cause and effect between dictatorship and communism not via the United States, but directly and inherently; for whatever may be said on the part played by the United States, the fact is that the mere existence of a dictatorship in a country acts inevitably as a preparation of that country for the advent of communism.

This is so obvious that it hardly needs elaboration. The dictator creates habits of submission without discussion to the powers that be. He is by necessity, if not by ideology (for which he does not care), a totalitarian. Used to an arbitrary totalitarianism, many of his subjects ripen into communists since, not unreasonably, they see in communism a totalitarian system which, at any rate, is dignified by an ideology.

Furthermore, most dictators, realizing the widespread fear of communism that afflicts the world, and in particular the United

States, seek to gain sympathy for their savage persecution of liberals, Christian democrats, socialists, by dubbing "communist" any and every political adversary they can collar. Hence, they present communism with the glory and aura of being the only or the leading party which seeks to liberate the country from its dictator.

Again, since the dictator proscribes all political parties, the only one that can thrive is the communist, for it possesses the best experience and training in clandestine activities and disposes of ample funds. In this way, a dictatorship finds itself in a kind of natural opposition-collaboration with communism; for even as the two stones of a mill collaborate by opposing one another, so the dictator and his country's communist party collaborate in opposition to grind out of existence the middle-of-the-way parties.

The conclusion is plain: The longer a dictator lasts the stronger grows the communist party of his country and the brighter its chances of success when the dictator falls.

This law has been illustrated to the full in Cuba, and to a lesser degree in Venezuela. The struggle of Rómulo Betancourt in Venezuela to save his country from communism is due to the growth of communism in that country under Pérez Jiménez. The ease with which Castro veered from a revolution which he presented as democratic to one the communist character of which is now undeniable was due to the long apprenticeship in totalitarianism inflicted on the Cuban people by Batista.

15.—THE ARMED FORCES

It is sometimes too readily assumed that the armed forces are probably the single most serious impediment to the development of democracy in Latin America. This would appear to be far too rash an assumption. It is true that most (though even here by no means all) of the dictators and tyrants Latin America had to suffer and every one of the present ones can be classed as "generals" in the sense described above; but leaving aside the fact that in not a few cases their gold braid was earned on the field of political rather than military battle, the fact is that the place of the armed forces in Latin American politics is a subject that should be considered apart from that of dictatorship.

There is in all Latin American armies a tradition of liberty which springs from the wars of emancipation from Spain. After all, it was from this struggle for independence, tinged as it was by tricolour ideologies and animated by echoes of the Marsellaise, that Latin American armies were born. San Martin and Bolívar were known in their time and are still known as the Liberators. Liberty is thus deeply etched into the tradition of the Latin American officer, and no precipitate conclusions should be drawn as to the motives and emotions behind this or that Latin American military coup. In 1957 the dictatorship of General Rojas Pinilla was ended by a military junta which gave way to the present liberal régime. In Honduras, in 1956, the dictatorship of President Lozano Diaz was ended by a military junta which gave way to the present liberal régime. And the whole world witnessed how General Aramburu, the leader who ultimately emerged from the military coup that ousted Perón, gave way to the present parliamentary régime. His prestige was so high when he acted as President that, had he stood as a candidate, his chances to win could have been overwhelming. He did not yield to the pressure exerted on him at the time by those who foresaw the troubles ahead, because he refused to tarnish the political disinterestedness of the military coup that had liberated the country from the dictator.*

*Though the idea is not identical, the view of a distinguished Colombian writer may be noted at this stage. "My theory [. . .] is quite simple. It seems to me that the army of [Latin] America is the only one in the world that was born to liberate peoples and not to conquer them. All the armies of Europe were set up in order to wrench some piece of land from the neighbouring country and to give the next neighbour to understand that he is being spied upon while preparations are being made to break his head. In America the armies are liberators. When San Martín passes the Andes and wins the battle of Chacabuco, which liberates Chile, the Chileans want to acclaim him as Governor, and he answers: 'Thanks, no. I came to help you win your liberty and not to gain a governorship.' Bolívar comes from Caracas to Upper Peru, liberates five republics and does not keep a single square inch of land." Germán Arciniegas in *Cuadernos*, No. 20, September-October 1956.

It is nevertheless a fact, of course, that in not a few cases the Army has been an anti-democratic element, particularly in countries where it was less of an institution and more like a glorified police force. In countries such as Chile and Argentina, the Army happens to be, today at any rate, a watchdog for democracy and, while discreetly in the wings, would almost certainly come out into the open if an attempt towards totalitarianism were made by extremists whether of the right or of the left. In Argentina, moreover, the Army runs secondary education establishments or high schools which, if the writer's experience can be generalized, are led by sincerely liberal men. Armies vary from one Latin American country to the other. In Colombia the Army is a modest, middle-class family of men of different ways of thinking, rather civilian-minded. In Venezuela it is more of a military caste. In Chile it is more intellectual; in Argentina, more political.

16. — CHANGE

Finally there is change. The scene is shifting. Not one of the features that have been briefly sketched but keeps moving and turning into something not quite the same. The rich are still too rich but getting less so; the poor still too poor but slowly rising. The middle class is increasing both in number and in powers; it is even becoming less averse to following technical professions. Indeed, a paradoxical phase has set in almost certainly temporary, in which young technicians trained at considerable expense by some Latin American nations are attracted by high salaries and opportunities to the United States. Such is often the case, for instance, with the young generation of Argentine technicians.

It is by no means certain that changes in university circles move all in the right direction. Here, unfortunately, the trend seems to be towards a stronger hold of faculties and students by Marxist philosophy and communist or philo-communist politics. Nevertheless, the trend is drawing out its countertrend, and the poison its antidote. Political stability is gaining ground, and the personal touch in politics is receding. Uruguay has given a courageous and original example by abolishing the presidency in favour of a Council in which the opposition is permanently represented. This is a somewhat extreme example and possibly a counsel of perfection; but the general trend is for parties to replace persons, though persons will probably still remain in Latin America a more weighty element in politics than in other countries. (Are they ever negligible in any?)

Imitation of the United States still goes on strongly; but as national consciousness increases it may recede. Obstacles to immigration are gradually yielding to commonsense. Standard of living and birth rate rise rapidly and this may help to correct the laxity of political institutions and to invigorate local public life. This, in its turn, would strengthen the State against present day encroachments by Army, Church, working class, capitalist or landowner. Much progress is noticeable in the attitude of foreign business; the welfare aspect of the enterprises is apt to be excellent, and a more intelligent understanding of the actual basis of co-operation between national and foreign interests is being attained.

All is changing, moving; and there is hope in the fact. But there is danger in it also. For the texture of the society that is moving is still weak and slack; and the circumstances favouring commonsense might find precisely in this change and in this movement an opportunity to upset the balance of it all.

17. — POLITICAL PARTIES

Such is the background on which a study of political parties in Latin America might be made. As a general observation, a word must be said on the imitative character of much of this party life. Party names are arbitrary enough everywhere, as the two chief labels in the United States suffice to prove, for who ever was able to define *republicans* and *democrats* otherwise than as the Montagues and Capulets of that huge Verona? In Latin America they bear a none too clear relation to the actual situation of the country in which they thrive. Nothing is less obvious than what some conservatives want to conserve unless it is the idea of liberty some liberals stand for, and so on along the line. There is the usual amount and more of personal feud behind splits and, more often than not, parties are conglomerates of family groups animated by family feuds and backed by local ownership of land, factory or commercial house.

Here again there is change; and not every party in every land can be said to be but a superstructure artificially erected over a more less passive mass. Cases in which real political life is sprouting from the earth will be observed as we proceed.

Argentina

The axis of Argentine political life has been for years the Radical Party, a conglomerate of middle-class intellectual, professional and business men, anti-clerical and more or less vaguely liberal. When Perón's dictatorship was ousted by a military coup animated by liberal and democratic tendencies, the Radical Party prepared itself to enter the lists and inherit power as soon as parliamentary institutions were restored. A scrupulous, possibly too scrupulous respect for the forms of democracy led the military junta headed by General Aramburu to hand over political control without securing first a change in the constitution that might have saved the country from demagogy.

The first impact of democratic life split the Radical Party, mostly on the attitude to adopt towards the austerity programme recommended by the best objective scientific advisers. The People's Radicals, led by Dr Balbin, declared in favour of such a programme; but a splinter group, led by Dr Arturo Frondizi, declared against. This split had a twofold consequence: together, the Radicals might have won, and therefore would have been able to constitute a government relatively independent of all other tendencies. Split, one or other of the fractions had to rely on alliances that would necessarily blur its campaign and jeopardize its future action. Dr Frondizi's critics claim that he sought, and (politically speaking) paid for the help of Roman Catholics, communists and Peronists. At any rate, he won, and since then has met with a number of difficulties that would appear to lend substance to his critics' claims. Whatever may be thought on this score, it is only fair to record his courage in adopting as President the austerity plans he had rejected as candidate, even if his fellow radicals of the Balbin persuasion may find his conversion rather belated.

To the right of both varieties of radicalism, a Conservative Party stands for the big landed and industrial interests; and further to the right, the Peronist Party, frankly fascist in its outlook and manners, keeps alive a threat to the peace and stability of the whole system. To the left, the social-democrats are socialists presenting a variety of hues with regard to their attitude to communism, from frankly anti-communist such as Americo Ghioldi to sympathizers, or at any rate neutrals, such as Alfredo Palacios. They are anti-Peronist; unlike a socialist group to their left, the Argentine Socialists, who are more orthodox in their Marxism but less disinclined to meet the Peronists at any rate on the trade-union or syndical field.

Further to the left, the Communist Party, led by Victorio Codovilla, is outflanked by Praxis, a group of Trotzkyite intellectuals whose leader is a brother of the President, Silvio Frondizi. Communism in Argentina penetrates most successfully the Arturo Frondizi-group within the radicals (*Radicales Intransigentes*), the university centres (both professors and students) and the Peronist syndicates, which, unlike the actual Peronist Party, must be considered in many ways as belonging to the left.

In the troubled circumstances of Argentine politics, a nation in which nearly one third of the population lives in the Buenos Aires conglomeration must be viewed as a mass potentially dangerous, and always exposed to communist intrigues, disorders and *coups*. The Army is at present a factor working for stability in the sense that it would not tolerate either a Peronist or a communist *coup*. Nevertheless, from the political point of view, the situation is not healthy insofar as it maintains the régime under a kind of military protectorate. The evolution towards the consolidation of liberal democracy would require an increase of the rural and provincial population and a devolution of powers to the provinces thus developed. The country is so rich in natural resources that a bold immigration policy would succeed if adequately prepared.

Chile

In Chile, the radicals are also the political axis of the country. They are divided if not split into three tendencies: right (Hernández), centre (Alfonso) and left, which was best incarnated by González Videla (President from October 1946 to 1952) thanks to the active help of the communists. Typically enough, Videla was not long in office before he had to initiate anti-communist measures which became stiffer and stiffer until the expulsion of communists from all public functions had to be decreed in 1948. But the pro-communist wing of the Radical Party, remains active and alive as it does in practically every "liberal" bourgeois party of Latin America.

To the right, the Christian Democrats are led by Senator Eduardo Frei; and there are two more parties further to the right, the Liberal and the Conservative.

To the left, there is a small national-popular group (Barrenechea) before we come to the FRAP or Popular Front. This is an uneasy alliance of socialists and communists, the first led by Dr Salvador Allende, the latter by Contreras Labarca; the latter would attract the radical left, the former would rather keep them out. There is a wing within the Socialist Party, led by Señor Ampuero, which would prefer less close ties with communism.

The situation is rendered more delicate by the fact that the dispossessed peasantry feel drawn to the FRAP, being persuaded that it is the only political group that would actually carry out an agrarian reform long overdue. That is why during the last presidential election, Dr Salvador Allende would have been elected if the parties of the right had not manoeuvred to reduce his votes by backing also a freak candidate, an ex-priest and demagogue who drew 41,000 votes from Dr Allende, just enough to set Dr Jorge Alessandri at the head of the poll with about 32,000 votes (4th September, 1958). A communist-socialist successful candidate to the presidency of Chile is not therefore to be excluded in 1964.

Here again, the question would then arise: what would the Army do? The Chilean Army is intelligent and liberal-minded. It is just possible that it might object to the access to power of communist Cabinet ministers. Nevertheless, the growing influence of communism among the students and intelligentsia is a factor to be reckoned with. One essential element would be to what extent a genuine land reform might enlarge the basis of contented citizens between now and then.

Peru

The establishment is strong above but clay-footed. Its power rests on economic rather than political force. It is not clear as to positive policy, and is moreover divided into factions which think differently and probably have opposite interests in matters such as inflation versus deflation. This is at present the governing sector, with roots in the landed and industrial oligarchy, the upper middle class, banking and trading circles. Their present man is President Manuel Prado; their future man is Dr Pedro Beltrán, the Prime Minister and Minister of Finance.

Practically every political colour that remains lies to the left of this governing group. The first is the Christian-Democratic Party, which appears to be ready for an agrarian reform bolder perhaps than anything that could be expected of the present team. It does not seem, however, to count on a considerable popular following.

Next on the left comes the Acción Popular led by a leader with considerable popular—his adversaries say, demagogic—gifts: Fernando Belaunde. He is ambitious and power-hungry and is credited with no particular inhibition as to eventual communist support. He was a close runner-up to President Prado in the last presidential election.

Further to the left we meet with APRA (*Alianza Popular Revolucionaria Americana*), the powerful popular movement founded by Victor Raul Haya de la Torre. This Movement for Revolutionary American Action began years ago as strongly revolutionary and anti-American; if never communist, not inimical to, though critical of, communism; and fiercely pro-Indian. It advocated calling Latin America Indo-America. APRA'S critics on the left, in particular the communists, reproach it for its newly acquired conservatism. Though not in office, it has been in power since the fall of the military dictator Odría (1956)—indeed more so than meets the eye, for its Secretary General, Señor Prialé, is held in all Peru as the power behind the throne.

To its left, the Peruvian Socialist Party, though relatively strong in the industrial north, is not a heavyweight in the political struggle on the national stage. The communists, on the other hand, are few but very active, keen and intelligent; and they have of late progressed considerably among the intellectual classes.

The situation in Peru may be described as more active perhaps without than within the parties. The best that could happen would be an alliance of APRA and the present conservative set-up on condition that the conservatives backed APRA for a sincere and thoroughgoing land reform. Otherwise, the Indians, who have heard of events in Bolivia, and travel there to see with their own astonished eyes, their brethren in command and possession of the land, may be aroused by some communist coup, which, politically, given the framework of the present system, might be successful.

Bolivia

The case of Bolivia is particularly interesting because it is perhaps the country in Latin America which has travelled farthest along the road to a real social, and not merely political revolution, even though at present the success of such a revolution may still be a matter for conjecture.

The leading party is the MNR (*Movimiento Nacionalista Revolucionario*). It won power twice, first democratically by winning the 1951 election, then by sheer violence when, excluded from power by a military junta, it fought its way to the summit in 1952. Its policy, whether spontaneous or dictated by events, is of an advanced socialist character. The three huge tin-mining estates (Patiño, Aramayo, Hochschild) have been nationalized. Had they been run with a more intelligent regard for the nation in which they were situated, their fate and that of Bolivia might have been better. As it is, the disorder and blunders to be expected from an operation carried out with more revolutionary ardour than competence, combined with wild fluctuations in the price of tin, plunged the country into chaos.

Under pressure from below, the MNR government set up an Agrarian Reform Council in 1953. The "reform" was already being carried out by armed bands of peasants. These events, as well as the practical wiping out of the Army as such and its replacement by formations of armed peasants and workers, gave the revolution a flavour somewhat reminiscent of the Soviets. The parallel should not be carried too far.

To the left of the MNR will be found the PIR (*Partido de Izquierda Revolucionaria*), Marxist but not communist, mostly in favour among university people; the Communist Party, led by Ramiro Otero, and a Trotzkyite party, the POR (*Partido Obrero Revolucionario*) split into the González and the Lora factions. All these parties to the left of the MNR do influence it, but no one could accuse the MNR leaders Victor Paz Estenssoro or Hernán Siles of being communists. Furthermore, the younger men of the party, already in the forefront, Guillermo Bedregal, Aníbal Aguilar Peñarrieta, Martin Alarcon Lahore, are by no means communists.

On the other side, the PURS (United Socialists) led by Enrique Herzog, the Liberal Party led by Montes, are moderate left; but the Falange Boliviana is a party as reactionary as its Spanish model and namesake, and is backed by Spanish clergy.

The prominent Labour leader is a Trotzkyite: Juan Lechín. It happens, however, that the COB (*Confederación Obrera Boliviana*), a kind of Trades Union Council, is gradually superseding the basic apparatus of MNR as sociological changes shift the centre of power towards workers and peasants. If, however, the Agrarian Reform is thoroughly carried out to its logical consequences, there would appear no danger in such a shifting of power from the MNR to the COB. What would be dangerous is if the land reform were frustrated and if such a failure came to be associated with the United States.

Ecuador

The middle zone in Ecuadorian political life is somewhat amorphous and may be more accurately described as an opinion than as a political party. The reason for this may well be the relative weakness of the middle class. It is from this zone that most presidents rise but on platforms seldom precise and even more seldom bold. Out of this political mist are seen to emerge two formations, one "liberal", whose exponent is Galo Plaza, the defeated candidate in the last general election, the other "conservative"; the former somewhat anti-clerical, the latter rather clerical and falangist.

There is a socialist party, which, though small, evinces two tendencies: a Marxist, philo-communist orientation, led by Manuel Agustin Aguirre, fairly successful in university circles, particularly in Quito and Cuenca; and a neutral socialism, led by Gonzalo Olea, more active among peasants and workers. Communism is led by Pedro Saad, an Ecuadorian of Arab origin.

Colombia

This country, which had for years, generations in fact, prided itself on being a model of peaceful constitutional government under the leadership of "doctors", went in recent years through an orgy of political murders amounting to civil war estimated by some observers at 250,000. Be it noticed, however, that this black period in her history was led and instigated by civilian "doctors", such as Ospina Pérez and Laureano Gómez, the former a conservative magnate, the latter a falangist politician who learnt his trade under Franco in Spain. The cadres of Gómez's dreaded police had been instructed in Franco-Spain.

Oddly enough, it was in order to put an end to the falangist-terrorist dictatorship of Laureano Gómez that the Army struck in 1953. There is in the Colombian Army an enlightened tradition of liberal democracy dating from the days of Generals Rafael Uribe and Benjamin Herrera. *General* Rojas Pinilla

seized power in 1953 and expelled *Dr* Gómez being then ac-
claimed by liberal opinion, very much as *Dr* Castro was when
he defeated *General* Batista. And in very much the same way
liberal opinion turned away from the saviour when it realized
that he followed very much the same ways as those of the tyrant
he had expelled.

But the new régime, though led by a fine liberal mind and a
generous spirit, President Lleras Camargo, does nevertheless
present some disquieting features. It amounts to an alliance between the liberals and not merely their adversaries, i.e., the
conservatives of a more or less democratic persuasion, but the
reactionary, falangist conservatives, led by Gómez. And what an
alliance! The liberals, who in the opinion of good observers
hold the majority in the country, have agreed to govern for
twelve years on a fifty-fifty basis of collaboration; an alternate
president, and an equal number of members of all representative bodies. Some observers in Colombia fear that, in accordance
with this arrangement, the next president will be Enrique
Gómez, Laureano Gómez's son, known for his falangist leanings.

Furthermore, the alliance implies the exclusion from public
life of any third political party. As for the press, a powerful,
centralized organization of publicity ensures that no paper but
those of the establishment can work. In these conditions, the
socialist trend breathes through the trades unions organizations,
of which there are two, the UTC (*Unión de Trabajadores
Colombianos*), confessional; and the CTC (*Confederación de
Trabajadores Colombianos*), strongly influenced by communists. The Communist Party (outlawed on 4th March, 1956)
works through the Movimiento Liberal Revolucionario, which
being led by Alfonso López, the son of a respected liberal leader
and President (now dead), is allowed to exist. This latitude
on the left is balanced by an equal latitude granted to the activities of a falangist Jesuit, Fr Felix Restrepo.

The resulting situation is unstable; and if a thoroughgoing
agrarian reform is not carried out to settle and stablilize the
peasant, a communist putsch could not be excluded.

Venezuela

Rómulo Betancourt holds the wheel of a vessel manned by a somewhat mixed and ill-assorted crew. His own Acción Democrática is led by Raul Leoni, and comprises socialist-democratic and liberal-democratic elements. To the right (?) the URD (*Unión Revolucionaria Democrática*), a middle-class movement, is led by an ambitious politician, Jóvito Villalba, in an opportunistic style which shows itself for instance in a pro-Castro attitude. This can have no other result than to expose Betancourt, who, with his usual courage, after backing Castro the liberator, denounced Castro the dictator. Further to the right, COPEI is the Christian-democratic group led by Rafael Caldera, and stands for conservative interests.

To the left of Acción Democrática, the Movimiento Izquierdista Revolucionario, led by a dynamic personality, Dionisio Alberto Rangel, stands for Marxist socialism and keeps its left-side door open towards communism.

There is a small but very active Communist Party led by snobbish wealthy men such as Otero Silva, a newspaper owner well fed on oil royalties, and the brothers Machado (Gustavo and Eduardo), trained in Moscow. This Communist Party of Venezuela does not willingly come out into the open. It works mostly through URD and MIR.

The weak elements in the situation are: an army which is more militant and more animated by a caste spirit than perhaps any other in Latin America, and strong enough to absorb 40 per cent of the budget; the huge unproductive load on the budget due to the army and to the need to satisfy the civil-service ambitions of a three-party government; the disloyal manoeuvering of some of the members or of parties which are in and out of the government at one and the same time; and a timid, all too timid attempt at solving the agrarian question. A communist attempt could not be excluded.

Paraguay

Two facts define the situation in Paraguay. One per cent of the population owns seventy-two per cent of the land; and a general is the unrestrained dictator of the country. His name is Alfredo Stroessner. He was the hero of the ultraconservatives (Colorados). Liberals, Febreristas (near-Socialists) and communists wait. So do the landless peasants. Liberation from some group of exiles has been rendered unlikely by the typically opportunistic policy of Dr Frondizi, of Argentina, who in October 1958 visited the dictator and showed him every form of friendship.

Brazil

The chief trouble in Brazil may well be the vagueness and amorphousness of its official political life and its divorce from the realities of the country. There is a *Travalhista* Party (a translation of "Labour Party" with no particular claim to resemble its British model in anything but label), which was the party of Getulio Vargas, and the Social-Democratic Party of General Teixeira Lott, with nothing to show in order to justify its two-barrelled title. Socialism is typically unrepresented, and communism is strong and well organized and well led on its political side by Luiz Carlos Prestes, on its cultural side by a writer of great prestige, Jorge Amado.

But, here again, the danger is the countryside. Landless peasants in the Parana region and in the north-east, in the region of Pernambuco, are getting restive. Peasant Leagues are sprouting everywhere; they become aggressive and will become highly dangerous if their claims are not met. The country is rich enough to weather the peril, but it will have to concentrate on it and neglect for the moment more spectacular expenditures. Communism is, for the time being, the most active political organized force in the land, and the organizer of the Pernambuco Peasant Leagues, Francisco Juliao, visited Moscow and Peking towards the turn of 1960-61.

This threat from the communist left may well have determined the foreign policy of President Quadros who, since his inauguration in January 1961, had shown signs of a rapid evolution to at least a neutralist attitude very close to the dividing line. A series of commercial and political approaches to the countries beyond the Iron Curtain including the Soviet Union, culminated in an invitation to Major Ernesto (Che) Guevara to visit Brazil. President Quadros went so far as to decorate him with the Grand Cross of the Southern Star. Accused of a conspiracy to turn his presidency into a totalitarian régime, he finally resigned on 25th August. There is some doubt as to whether he expected his resignation to be accepted.

After a tug of political war between right and left, dominated by the armed forces, and in order to spare the country a civil war, the Constitution was wisely altered so that the organization of the country became more parliamentarian and less presidential. This, up to a point, reduces the risks of a communist-minded president delivering the country to the other side, as has happened in Cuba. But the danger remains.

Other South and Central American countries

I shall not deal in any detail with *Uruguay* because it is a country in which the usual difficulties that beset Latin American countries, if not altogether absent, are very much attenuated. Differences between rich and poor, landownership, illiteracy are here present but in a minor key. A kind of State socialism is spreading, which tends unduly to increase a not very productive bureaucracy. The usual flirtation with Moscow among the intelligentsia is perhaps less acute. But Montevideo is one of the two chief centres of Soviet activity in the Spanish-speaking world.

In such a setting, parties do not mean very much, beyond a network of almost family relationships. As an indication of their relative strength, the figures may be given of the votes for the respective candidates for the presidential council on 28th November, 1954. *Colorado* Party (vaguely liberal): 387, 803; *Blanco* Party (vaguely conservative): 266,960; Civic Union (Catholic): 27,929; Socialist: 26,368; Communist: 17,773. The first two stand respectively for the Batlle and the Herrera families.

Costa Rica bears some comparison with Uruguay in that it is also a small, nearly all-white, liberal country. Under the leadership of José Figueres, who ousted a dictator, Teodoro Picado, in 1948, the small republic has abolished its army, keeping only a kind of internal order national militia, the Civic Guard.

To the north, *Nicaragua* is the estate of the Somoza family, whose ascent to power followed the murder of the anti-American leader Sandino. Anastasio Somoza, the elder, ruled the country with an iron hand either directly or through his nominees from 1935 until his own murder on 29th September, 1956, at the hands of a student. Owning the land, its business, its government, its police and its newspapers, as well as the not even discreet friendship of the United States, it was child's play for his son Luis Somoza to follow his father.

Honduras. Here again, parties had not meant very much until the rebirth of the Liberal Party under young leaders aware of the need for social change. The long, brutal dictatorship of General Carías ended in 1948 when he himself handed on office (though not, as he meant it, power) to Dr Juan Manuel Gálvez. When the new President's term expired (in 1954) the election went in favour of the liberal leader, Dr José Ramón Villeda Morales; but Gálvez's Vice-President, Julio Lozano, seized power and declared a "constitutional dictatorship". This did not please the army, and on 21st October, 1956, the usurper was overthrown by a military *coup*. In 1957, the junta held an election, and Villeda Morales, elected, took office.

The biggest economic forces in the land are the United Fruit Company and the Standard Fruit and Steamship Company. Neither dictatorships nor liberal governments, generals nor doctors can govern without them, still less against them.

El Salvador is a small republic owned by a rich class. The party in power is named Revolutionary Party of Democratic Union, a name in which probably the only word meaning what it says is "Party". The chief problem, here as everywhere in Latin America, is whether, and if so, when and how, the agrarian reform will take place.

Mexico

Of all Latin American nations, Mexico is the most advanced

on the road towards a real social as well as political democracy. This fact, as well as her population (31 million), much higher than that of the next most populated Spanish-speaking nation in the area (Argentina, 20 million), as well as her proximity to the United States, make Mexico one of the key countries in the New World.

After the dramatic disorders of the first years of the revolution begun in 1910, this fertile movement gained a weight and a responsibility it had sadly lacked at first, with the advent of Venustiano Carranza, who wisely wrote land reform into the new (1917) constitution as one of the chief aims of the new State.

Since then, Mexico has achieved a remarkable success in every walk of life. The oil interests were nationalized without bringing about a break with the United States; a formidable agrarian reform has been carried out; a campaign for the building of schools and the reduction of illiteracy has been fruitful and continues in full swing; the level of public health has risen considerably (which in part explains Mexico's dramatic rise in population); a number of prosperous new industries have been started; and, last but not least, a remarkable measure of political stability has been achieved.

It would nevertheless be unwise to conclude that there is no communist danger in Mexico. A number of circumstances are disquieting. The first is that for a set of causes of the utmost complexity, the actual power of the President goes far beyond his constitutionally defined scope. "An amalgam of Spanish Viceroy and Aztec conqueror", as it was put to me once by an acute Mexican observer, the Mexican President is the source of all actual power; and it would be possible for an occupier of the post to steer the boat in the wrong direction. That such an event lies within the bounds of possibility is proved by the mere existence of General Lázaro Cárdenas, who was President in the nineteen-thirties, and is now a staunch ally of Moscow, who has retained a considerable hold of the country and an almost feudal omnipotence in the State of Michoacán.

The second is that the very system into which the revolution has in the end set conforms to the pattern of a one-party régime. One or two other parties exist but only on sufferance. The one that counts is the Partido Revolucionario Institucional. To it belong the men that govern, the votes, the springs of power; and through a skilful use of such springs, in fact, if not in law, also the press. This state of affairs results, at any rate in Mexico, in a situation of internal peace and progress; but it does accustom the people to be governed by one party with one man at the top. That would appear to be an easy way to communism.

The third disquieting circumstance is that, though sincerely democratic and jealous of its liberty, the party in power and its men do not seem inclined openly to quarrel with the communists. There are in fact within the party cordial and active, one might almost say militant collaborators with communism, and the activities of such fellow-travellers as ex-President Cárdenas and Lombardo Toledano, the labour leader, find no bars and no checks.

In conclusion, though the Mexican situation would appear to allow some optimism when compared with nearly every country to the south, it should be carefully watched.

Conclusion

This rapid survey of the political situation in Latin America* must at first sight suggest a good deal of variety and dispersion. It is nevertheless not altogether lacking in unity. Everywhere we find political uncertainty and even in some cases instability; conditions on the whole favourable to communism; and a land question which must be solved and is not being solved.

This last circumstance is dangerous in a twofold way: it keeps vast quantities of men unsatisfied, at a time when they are becoming daily more aware of their condition as dispossessed and neglected citizens; and it swells the urban proletariat with masses of uprooted men who are ready to follow any demagogic lead.

The picture would not be complete without some reference to the film. Hollywood bids fair to be and to have been the most

*The Dominican Republic and Haiti as well as Guatemala will be discussed in a later chapter.

potent source of revolutionary ferment in the world. The film is the book of the illiterate. It has taught them things undreamt of in their experiences. Millions of simple beings lost in their villages had never as much as imagined how a rich man lived. Hollywood brought to their astounded eyes the lavish life of the rich, and with a vengeance. Why should I go on lying on my mat of lice? asks the illiterate Indian. And so he goes to swell the mass of those whose sons will avidly devour cheap leaflets and pamphlets from Moscow. That the film comes from the United States only adds mustard to the sauce.

The problem as a whole would then appear to be how to bring about in the whole of South America a fairly rapid change similar at least to that which Mexico has achieved, without falling into one of two extremes: the too cautious approach (on the present Venezuelan lines, for instance) which might frustrate the peasants, or a riotous, disorderly revolution which might lead either to a new wave of dictatorships or to a number of communist victories, disastrous for the world situation.

II

THE SPANISH ASPECT

I.—GENERAL OBSERVATIONS

THE average American reader may raise his eyebrows. What—he will ask—has Spain to do in this business? Such is the extent to which some of the deep-lying, vital elements of our problem are neglected or overlooked. This is one of the negative attitudes on the part of general, mis-informed opinion in the United States towards those described (absurdly enough) as "the Latins". Little progress can be made in the field of inter-American relations unless the people of the United States endeavour to get rid of their anti-Spanish prejudices. Indifference, ignorance, contempt are by no means sound materials for a solid bridge between the two Americas; yet, at present, few better materials seem to be available. Awkward as the task may be, we must therefore begin by examining this prejudice.

It is not easy to be a Spaniard. The load of history one has to carry is heavy enough. The load of legend is even heavier. France, Italy, Britain, the Netherlands, all the protestant North of Europe, the United States and Spanish America have a vested interest in adding to the weight. Wherever he turns, the Spaniard finds not merely stern critics, whom he need not particularly fear, since he is no worse than any of them, but strongly prejudiced minds and hearts, the stronger for their self-ignorance on the score. With few, though luminous exceptions, it is impossible to open a book or see a film or a play having anything to do with Spain without reading wild generalizations couched in violent terms still redolent of the days of cut-throat enmity between "Christian" nations which lent so much dramatic interest to the sixteenth and seventeenth centuries. Qualifications and appeals to a sense of proportion, to historical limitations, to the shortcomings of the age and similar counsels of moderation—frequent enough when discussing the English in Ireland, the Dutch in Asia, the Americans in Mexico—vanish when the theme happens to be the Spaniards in the Netherlands or in Spanish America. And nothing remains but such epithets as "bloodthirsty" and "gold-hungry" to describe one of the most creative empires the world has known.*

The discovery of America was a disaster for Spain, and possibly for Europe as well. It was a pity that things did not happen otherwise. America should have been discovered by the English, which is what might have happened if Ferdinand and Isabel had locked up Columbus in a lunatic asylum where he belonged. That formidable reservoir of human energy which went west and mastered a continent in a generation should have invaded the southern shores of the Mediterranean, from Tangiers to the Bosphorus. The Spanish-American nations would today be Spanish-African; the whole of America would be an English-speaking continent; and France, free in Europe, would have spread her culture from Paris to Moscow in peace. Spain was deflected from her true course, and torn between a western call on her energy and northern activities which, contrary to her real interests, were imposed on her people by the dynastic interests of her kings.

Two pairs of naïve contradictions seem to govern the rough and ready opinions which lurk at the back of most people's minds about Spain. The Spaniards wiped out the population of

*A few examples: Spanish names are avoided by historians and librarians. Colón (for such was his name and so he wished to be known) became Columbus or Colombo, with ludicrous results as to how to file his sons and grandsons. Borja becomes Borgia, Espinosa (for so he signed himself) becomes Spinoza and Portuguese. Domenico Scarlatti called himself Domingo Escarlate in Spain but the rule that made Borja into Borgia works the other way for him. *Fidelio* of Beethoven is based on an historical episode which happened in France, but as there is a dungeon and a chorus of prisoners, over it went to Spain. And so on.

Spanish America and then exploited it ruthlessly for three centuries; the Spaniards impoverished their "colonies" and "plundered" them though by the time these colonies rebelled they were far richer than the mother country.

Now, when we come closer to the facts we find that perhaps with the single exception of the Roman, no other empire in history, not even the British, succeeded in rooting its civilization and culture right into the very core of the peoples it invaded as the Spanish empire did.

Since I have dealt with this matter to the best of my ability elsewhere,* I shall here limit my observations on the general historical aspect of the subject to the conclusions that can be confidently drawn.

(*a*) Contrary to what is still sometimes asserted, the three great native civilizations which were superseded by the Spanish rule—the Aztec, the Inca, and the Chibcha—were barbarous, and in many ways terrible, and their disappearance brought immense benefit to the New World. In what concerns New Spain, the change struck a man as passionately devoted to the interests of the natives as Father Motolinia:

> In this new Spain there were constant big wars, in which those of some provinces fought against those of others, and many died both in the fights and as prisoners sacrificed to their demons. Today [February, 1541] through the kindness of God, they are all converted in such peace and quiet, and with so much justice, that a Spaniard or a boy can carry a load of ingots of gold three hundred and four hundred leagues, by hills and mountains, through populated or unpopulated land, with no more fear than if he went through the main street of Benavente [the friar's birthplace in Spain].

(*b*) *There was nothing especially and exceptionally cruel about the Spanish conquest and colonization.* There was indeed

---

*The Rise of the Spanish American Empire, and *The Fall of the Spanish American Empire,* New York, The Macmillan Co, London, Hollis and Carter, 1947.

abominable cruelty, especially at first, in the Antilles, and also right through the three centuries in certain places and aspects of the life of the Indies. But such cruelty as there was can by no means be considered as abnormal, given the standards of the time, the ways of other nations, the novelty of the historical situation and the psychological forces let loose by the meeting of the two worlds.

(*c*) What was exceptional was the very opposite: that, as a State, Spain set her face against all ill-treatment of Indians and blacks, severely punished it in her laws, and despite many and grave errors and inconsistencies, saved and developed the Indian population and evolved a system of relations with the blacks which, though far from perfect, was better than—or not so bad as—the French, the English, the Danish or the Dutch.

(*d*) Spain evolved towards the new peoples under her sway an original attitude born of her own political conceptions and religious faith, and was both constructive and far in advance of her time. This attitude was rooted in the following principles and beliefs:

1. On the political side, the implicit but definite recognition of separate personalities for each one of the kingdoms of the Indies, and the blend of autocratic-theocratic forms with democratic forms of political law, not excluding native political traditions.

2. On the religious side, the recognition of the equality of all men before God, whatever their caste or colour.

(*e*) The Inquisition came late, was insistently asked for by the American Kingdoms, and in three centuries sacrificed rather less than ninety victims for the whole continent, i.e., about one every three years.

(*f*) The inflow of books was huge and education far more fostered in breadth and in depth than in Spain or indeed anywhere in Europe.

(*g*) Though there was a good deal of centralization in the Crown, whose power was exerted through the Council of the

Indies and the Viceroys, municipal democracy was strong. This became manifest when the Cabildo, or municipal council of the chief city of each territory or "kingdom", assumed national sovereignty and led it to independence along lines in conformity with Spanish municipal law. Furthermore, the slowness of communications in the days of the sail and the mule were an efficient antidote to any centralization, and the general criticism throughout the three centuries was not that there was not enough liberty but rather that there was too much.

(*h*) Economically, the mistakes made were those every European Kingdom was making at the time; but it is not true that Spain "never forgot for one moment that the purpose of the colonies was to provide wealth for the mother country". The American Kingdoms had their own personalities on a footing of equality with the European Kingdoms of the Crown of Spain; sometimes the interest of one, sometimes that of the other, had more weight at Court. Furthermore, sometimes one American country was sacrificed to another American country that happened to be stronger. Thus the long sacrifice of Buenos Aires as a port was by no means due to Spain, who would certainly have benefited if the absurd system of trading via Panama-Lima had been abolished. But Panama and Lima were too strong at Court.

(*i*) The humane activity of the friars was admirable, and the natives were never forgotten in the matter of hospitals.

(*j*) What oppression there was (never worse than that which other nations inflicted at the time, or even later, on their wards) was on the whole not oppression of the Indian Kingdoms by the Crown of Spain, but of Indians and blacks by whites and their *mestizo* and half-caste servants, in violation of standing Spanish laws. The responsibility for this oppression rested on the Creole whites and on the Spanish-born whites settled in the Indies on business or as officials of the Crown. Some responsibility must go to the Crown also, since the system of selling offices, which reached its maximum towards 1650-1700, stimulated corruption and ill-treatment of the natives. With this grave reservation, the Crown may be said to have been the staunchest

protector of the Indians. Oppression of white Creoles was practically unknown. Such things as the French *Lettre de Cachet,*
the English *Star Chamber* and other forms of arbitrary
imprisonment or persecution by the Crown or its Viceroy for
capricious or tyrannous motives were on the whole unknown in
the Indies.

(*k*) Despite the relentless enmity of the strongest and ablest
European powers, the Empire lived three centuries which count
in History as one of the most creative, and certainly the most
peaceful, a continent has ever known.

Three final observations: at the end of the three centuries
of Spanish rule, there were more natives than at the beginning; at that period, the Spanish Kingdoms were rich and their
money was the most sought after currency in the world; finally,
in the words of a distinguished Venezuelan historian: "Never
in more than a century of independent life has Venezuela produced a better élite than that evolved by what the literature of
our declaimers was until recently describing as the black night
of colonial ignorance."*

2. — PENETRATION OF SPAIN

One of the most baffling features of this Spanish era of
America was the rapidity and the depth of its penetration in so
vast and forbidding a continent. Let us leave aside the Conquest
and what is perhaps even more astounding, the process of discovery and consolidation of the huge continent. For our purpose, what matters most is the cultural penetration, as mani-
fested in religion, language and ways of living. It is important to
point out that the vehicle for both religion and ways of living,
i.e., the language, must have spread on its own merits so to
speak, for the Church, which did most of the work in this field,
was by no means willing to act as a propagator of Spanish, and
preferred her priests and friars to learn the vernaculars.

Nevertheless, the language took root so deeply that it is found

*C. Parra Pérez, *Historia de la Primera República de Venezuela,*
Caracas, 1939, pp. 356-7.

everywhere, even alongside the relatively small pockets of vernacular left here and there to this day. Where wider groups have remained ignorant of Spanish (as in Bolivia) a considerable number of Spanish terms and ways has nevertheless infiltrated their culture.*

Similar conclusions may be drawn from a recent account of a survey of the near-extinct Noanama Indians on the banks of the river San Juan near the Colombian Pacific seaboard.†

The Anglo-Colombian expedition notes that the "Noanama, once a populous tribe of the Chocó and related to the Cariban culture of the Atlantic coast, unlike many other tribes had little contact with the early Spanish *conquistadores*. Although now numbering only about 1,000 persons, they are a people who still retain their own way of life and culture in spite of their proximity to Buenaventura, the influence of the Negroes who live alongside them and Catholic missionaries." Nevertheless, most of the words quoted by the expedition to describe things such as *trapiche* (sugar cane press), *guarapo* (a drink), *rastrojo* (a garden), *velorios* (funeral chants), *batea* (a basin) are Castilian.

A few personal experiences may round up this rapid survey. During my first visit to Cuzco, many years ago, a mestizo professor of Cuzco University who was showing me the city suddenly hailed a lean, tall Indian of about fifty and asked him in Quechua: "Who are you?" The man gave his name and volunteered to add : "I belong to Don Bartolomé González." He knew perhaps no Spanish; but I had noticed the clothes he was wearing: they were a fairly faithful though shabby version of the Court dress worn in Spain towards 1770.

During that same visit, I was offered an evening entertainment at the residence of the Spanish Consul General in Lima.

---

*This is patent in "La Conception de L'Ame et de la Maladie Chez les Indiens d'Amerique" by Jehan Vellard, in *Revue de Psychologie des Peuples*, 4ème Trimestre, 1960, also, though perhaps not so directly, in Bolivia: "U.S. Assistance in a Revolutionary Setting" by Richard W. Patch in *Social Change in Latin America Today*, New York, 1960, Harper and Brothers, for the Council on Foreign Relations.

†*The Times*, London, January 1st, 1961.

I was travelling as Spanish Ambassador at large on a special mission to four Spanish American countries, including Peru. The chief attraction was a display of Indian dancing by a boy and a girl, to music played on an old Indian instrument by their father. It was really delightful. But the harp was an archaic Spanish harp and the three performers, father, daughter and son, wore Spanish (very old fashioned) garments. Furthermore, the musician, having heard me described as *Embajador,* must (my friends and I assumed) have understood it more or less vaguely as *Emperador* and never consented that I should see his back. When he finally left the room he walked backwards.

Many years later, during my third visit to Peru, I was invited to attend an evening of Inca folklore in Cuzco. It was commented upon and explained by a young, intelligent mestizo. I saw nothing that had not come from Spain, and most of what I heard was Spanish also.

The fact is that in matters of dress and folklore no less than in religion, language and ways of living, Spanish America is, of course, deeply Spanish. And this is not being insisted upon here out of a nationalism which would be as silly as it would be obsolete; but because it is both an essential and a far too often forgotten aspect of the situation.

Since from the very first days of the Conquest, the Spaniard has known no colour bar and has mixed his blood with that of the natives, Spanish America is essentially a mestizo country. This applies, though in a lesser degree, to the Río de la Plata republics, for the extermination of the Indians in Argentina did not take place until the middle of the nineteenth century.

The two poles of the Spanish American character will therefor be the Spaniard and the Indian. It is, I believe, a mistake to endeavour to contrast mestizo and Indian,* for in that way the comparison is blurred and confused. The mestizo is the conveyor of the Spanish culture to the Indian. Though in itself his culture is entitled, up to a point, to an autonomous treatment, what he stands for when confronted with the Indian is Spanish

*As for instance in some of the otherwise remarkable essays in *Social Change in Latin America Today* already quoted.

culture. It becomes necessary, therefore, to study the Spanish element in Spanish America for this study will reveal the roots of much that we have already observed in Spanish American life and ways of living.

3. — THE SPANISH CHARACTER

The Spaniard is a European.* The chief characteristic of the European is the predominance of the individuated faculties of the spirit—intellect and will—over the collective ones (instinct and intuition). Furthermore, there is in him a close relationship between these two faculties, for his intelligence is active and his will is intelligent. Knowledge in the European is not contemplative or disinterested; it is acquisitive and enterprising. His will is no mere impulse towards action, but an active move fully conscious of its immediate and ultimate scope. Finally, in the European the two faculties are balanced.

European life borrows its chief features from these basic characteristics of the European. It is, to begin with, individualistic, for mind and will are the individuated faculties of man. In its turn, this explains the force of the two chief traditions in European life, the Socratic and the Christian; the Socratic tradition stands for freedom of thought; the Christian tradition guarantees the integrity of the human person. The first serves truth; the second, charity.

This individualistic spirit of the European leads to his feeling for quality. Live is qualitative. Quantity is merely mineral. Individuation is unthinkable not merely without quality but without uniqueness. Every man and woman in the world is unique.

Quality in its turn leads to a non-utilitarian attitude. We have seen that knowledge in the European is not contemplative but acquisitive. As a first move, therefore, the European is utilitarian, but not ultimately. His real aim is leisure and the full

*I have dealt with European psychology in *Portrait of Europe*, Hollis and Carter, London, 1952, and with Spanish psychology in *Englishmen, Frenchmen, Spaniards*, Oxford University Press, London.

flavour of life and of the intimate knowledge that flows from living.

Finally, the European's play of will-intellect is apt to manifest itself in a three-beat rhythm: the will going out to seize hold of the object, soon overtaken by the intellect that seeks to reduce the anarchy of the will to an intelligent order; and finally, a synthesis of both faculties in the third and last phase. This rhythm can be observed in science (fact-finding—hypothesis—synthesis); in politics (anarchy—monarchy—democracy); in European expansion (discovery and conquest—colonization—emancipation).

The Spaniard as a European presents all these characteristics in his own special way as also do other Europeans, each in his own way. Shallow observers will, no doubt, tend to see the strength of the Spaniard's will more readily than that of his intellect. I believe this to be an error, though explicable, as I hope to show anon. The Spaniard is one of the most intelligent of European peoples; as well as one of those in whose midst intelligence is distributed most equitably. This fact is in itself one of the chief obstacles for political stability, for social indiscipline is the inevitable outcome of too little intellectual inequality between the leaders and the led.

We are now entering the zone of the shades that single out the Spaniard among his fellow Europeans. There are two components in every human will: one, which might be described as "horizontal", acts in inter-human relations, works through human institutions and weaves the tissue of collective actions; the other, which we might call "vertical", seeks the summit of individual life, universal, diabolic or divine, and by its very orientation avoids the community and yearns to rise above the individual. The shade that separates the Spaniard from the other Europeans consists in this: that in his will the vertical component is far stronger than the horizontal.

A number of features of the Spanish character which passed on to the Spanish American can be deduced from this. The Spaniard is, for instance, the least utilitarian of Europeans. A typical Spanish remark when witnessing a man found too active and agitated for the good of his soul: "And all that, in order to become a dead man."

This strong vertical component of the Spanish character might also account for his religious attitude, quite apart from the particular form of confession he happened to be born in, or had chosen. For the vertical component is religious and the horizontal component is moral, since the former yearns towards God and the latter spends itself among one's neighbours. Hence, perhaps, the Spaniard's fidelity to Catholicism which, in fact if not in theory, is the most religious and vertical, the least moral and horizontal of the Christian confessions. Under the influence of the Enlightenment and its aftermath throughout the nineteenth and twentieth centuries, a good half of Spain has lost sympathy with the outward forms of the Catholic religion. It is nevertheless doubtful whether the outcome can be compared with French Jacobinism or Italian scepticism. What remains is too complex for a rapid analysis, but might be summed up in that famous Spanish answer to the question: What is your religion?—I am an atheist, thank God.

For similar reasons, the Spaniard has a profound *universal* sense. It would appear at first sight that the direct line to universality would be the horizontal rather than the vertical component of the spirit, which leads to municipal, national, worldwide interests in a series of concentric circles. Yet, this way bristles with obstacles. Every circle is a ditch or a wall. The vertical component, as happens in artillery, by firing high, reaches the far distant horizon instantly and freely. In his human relations, the Spaniard is the most universal of Europeans.

Might we not adumbrate here some of the causes of that neglect of science which is yet another of the shadings that singles out the Spaniard among Europeans? Not a little of the disdain in which Spanish culture is held in Anglo-Saxon circles comes from this feature. Science, at any rate its technological and analytical aspects (which hold sway nowadays), belongs to the horizontal set of man's activities. Technology means control over matter. It requires patience and objectivity, horizontal virtues not prominent in the Spaniard. When Ortega, an advocate of horizontal virtues, complained of the lack of inventions in Spanish scientific history, Unamuno (a verticalist) retorted: "Let them invent!", meaning by "them" the other Europeans, and he praised above all scientific inventions the mystical intuitions of St John of the Cross, the swiftest rising skylark in our skies.

This shrinking from science, particularly in its practical and technical aspects, has been scored against Spain often enough. It would suffice to define Europe as the continent of science to be able to expel Spain from Europe unjustly but not without some appearance of plausibility, and in fact it has been done more than once. The view has been put forward that the civilization which the Spaniards brought to the New World was not their own but that which they had imported from Europe across the Pyrenees. This view is worth considering if only to bring out the two errors on which it rests.

The first is an error of fact. Let us grant that such things as nuclear science, modern electrical and aviation marvels owe little to Spain (even though in air navigation La Cierva was a first-rate pioneer who would have been less swiftly forgotten had his name been Doe, Labiche or Hindin). Nevertheless, the discovery and conquest of America were carried out on Spanish technique, and in a European spirit in what concerns thirst for knowledge. For centuries European seamen used navigation treatises such as *El Arte de Navegar* by Pedro de Medina or *Breve Compendio* by Martin Cortés.* Who but the Spaniards discovered the great sea lanes? Who circumnavigated the world for the first time? Who studied the newly discovered countries with a keener curiosity, both human and scientific? Cortés could not pass by the volcanoes without sending an expedition to study them. His reports to Charles V are models of intelligent observation. Hardly established in the New

---

*It is both a duty and a pleasure to record here how much Spain owes to the work of American specialists on this subject, and in particular to Professor Haring of Harvard.

World, the Spaniards originated a regular stream of books at once on the countries, peoples, fauna and flora, language and customs of the lands they were discovering. The Crown organized questionnaires for collecting information which deserve the admiration of the modern sociologist for their all-round and intelligent curiosity. Spaniards developed the mining and metallurgical industries and invented processes for the extraction of metals.

All this did not prevent that monument of encyclopaedic knowledge and universal incomprehension, H. G. Wells, from writing: "It is a misfortune for science that the first Europeans to reach America were these rather uncurious Spaniards, without any scientific passion, thirsting for gold, and full of the blind bigotry of a recent religious war. They made few intelligent observations of the native methods and ideas of these primordial people. They slaughtered them and baptized them; but they made small note of the customs and motives that changed and vanished under their assault."* Poor Wells was thoroughly ignorant of this as of many other subjects; knowing no language but English, he had never heard of Sahagún, who wrote his *Historia de Las Cosas de Nueva España* within the lifetime of Cortés, with such a sense of scientific observation that he must be considered as the founder of anthropology, nor of Sarmiento de Gamboa, Durán, Monardes and many more scientific observers of men, nature and plants, and if he had heard of Torquemada, the acute observer of the *Monarquia Indiana*, he would probably have mistaken him for the Inquisitor.

There is perhaps in all this lamentable attitude towards Spain more ignorance than malevolence. And in this way we come to the second error of the tendency to define Europe as the continent of science. It is far too narrow an idea of Europe, for it leaves out the Christian tradition and reduces the Socratic tradition to applied science and know-how. Now, it is plain to any impartial observer of the facts of Spain's American history that in their treatment of the Indians, if far too many individual

The Outline of History, first ed. 1920, p. 408; seventh ed., 1933, p. 776.

Spaniards sinned abominably, the system did not sin; that the Crown was ever anxious to defend and protect them; that when they suffered, it was nearly always due precisely to the distance and the looseness of the chain of power, i.e., to excess of liberty rather than lack of liberty in the kingdoms beyond the seas, and that at the end of the Spanish period there were more natives than at the beginning.

So that, in conclusion, if, on the score of their American history, the Spaniards on the Day of Reckoning will have to cast down their eyes before the Lord, on earth today they can look straight in the eyes of any other people.

4. — NATIONS-WHO AND NATIONS-WHAT

Fortunately the Lord has made many peoples, and some this way and some that. If we reduce our observation to the European family, and if we imagine them all sitting round a table, on which an angel has thrown a problem, the peoples of Europe will react in two different ways. The North-West will want to know *what* is to be done; the South-East will want to know *who* is to do it. Let us now qualify. All will want to know the what and the who of it; but Scandinavians, Britons and Swiss will stress the *what;* Greeks, Italians and Spaniards the *who;* and the others will vacillate. Of the *who*-peoples, the "whoest" are the Spaniards.

Put in other words, some Europeans are more interested in the public thing, others in the public person. Thing, in Latin *res.* The public-thing-peoples are therefore republicans; the public-man-peoples are monarchists. Since public life consists mainly in solving public things as you go along, it follows that republican peoples (in our sense of the word, i.e., realistic, objective) are those most likely to carry on peacefully; while monarchist (i.e., personalist, subjective) peoples will more likely be exposed to an agitated political life. Therefore, the first condition for any form of government to work smoothly is for the people to be "republican", i.e., objective, realistic, what-people; no matter whether the actual form of their government is a monarchy or a republic and no matter which of the two *forms* they prefer.

By and large, the Spaniards are a "people-who". And so are the Spanish Americans. Whether you are in a parliament, a law court, a bank, a theatre, a night club or a shop, the chief thing is to find the Don Fulano* who runs it. Spanish, and therefore, Spanish American things, are apt to be one-man shows to a far greater degree than is the case in other human families.

5. — THE CAPE-AND-SWORD AND THE GOWN

This by no means should be taken to imply that the *republican*, i.e., the objective, element was absent in Spanish America during the vice-regal period. It was in fact often present and active, and the point is worth considering owing to its bearing on present day types and events.

Spain sent to "the Indies" as governors two types of men, styled, respectively, viceroys and presidents. The chief difference between them was one of rank. The viceroys were cape-and-sword men, scions of the nobility and therefore knights, or, as we should say today, military men. The presidents were lawyers and clerics, which in those days often went together, gown-men. The dividing line could be blurred now and then, and a knight be bookish-minded and a prelate warlike, but the distinction is nevertheless substantial.

It sprang from roots deeply buried in the subsoil of character. The cape-and-sword man was a nobleman whose acts sprang from temper and boldness, whose norm was honour, whose justification was apt to be after the event. "Yes. I've done it because I've done it. My honour is in it. If you don't agree, here is my life which I risk for my name."

The gown-man sprang nearly always from a lower middle class or peasant family, had been educated on public, church or nobleman's charity, and stood on what was objectively right. He justified his actions before, not after the event. In case of conflict, he would appeal to the courts.

*Fulano = So-and-So.

These two prototypes stood for the monarchist and the republican spirit respectively, in the sense outlined above of these words, i.e., for the subjective and the objective, the *a posteriori* and the *a priori* justification of behaviour. They were aptly called viceroy and president, for they stood in a way each for one of the two forms of government, the monarchist and the republican.

It will be readily understood that these two forms of leadership in the Indies were respectively associated with the *who* and the *what* types of government and that, therefore, there was and is in the Spanish world a strong natural tendency towards the *who*-type, i.e., the viceroy. But the matter may be taken one step farther; for it is also plain that these prototypes —*who*-viceroy, *what*-president—prolong themselves into our present world (see Chapter 1, section 6) in the contrast between generals and doctors; so that the pattern would be *who*-viceroy-general versus *what*-president-doctor.

It may at first sight seem odd that in this team it was the Church that stood for what we would today call democracy; but such was the case; for the churchman felt two republican springs in him: one was the spirit of equality breathed in the Gospels; the other one was his own origin which often was humble, so that the Church (and the Law) was then in Spain a democratic ladder that raised humble men to the summits of power.

Although in modern days the Church has forsaken this democratic tradition, the Law, a kind of lay church, has kept it alive; and such is the root of the "doctor" type in Spanish American affairs, as opposed to the "general" type, which hails back to the cape-and-sword man and the viceroy.

6. — INSTITUTIONS AND LAWS

This contrast provides the mainspring for public life in the Spanish American Kingdoms which have today become the Spanish American nations. For it might be said without excessive simplification that legislation came from the gown-man-republican-president spirit and the way it was applied or dodged from the cape-and-sword-monarchist-viceroy spirit. No attempt should be made to group all viceroys this way and all presidents that way of the dividing line. It is a matter of attitude rather than of men. The chief point is that the *Leyes de Indias* are wise, human, liberal and humane; and that whenever abuses, crimes, atrocities were committed, they were sins against the system, acts of anarchy. Nor should one forget that conflict is heard of oftener than peace, and that, by and large, the situation was bad only here and there at this or that time.*

The influence of the theologians gave rise to a number of features which bear on present-day matters as described in Chapter 1. Education was widespread and from the first sought to enlighten the native. It was universal rather than national; and the classics read were those of antiquity and not those of Spain.

Here may be found the roots of a number of Spanish American features noted in a previous section. Thus the subtler minds one is apt to find in the South; their more pronounced tendency to general ideas and their disinclination for the merely utilitarian; their all-too-frequent proclivity to literary form, including verse; their dislike of technical work (features which may be considered at will as positive or negative), arise from these three centuries of a scholastic, generally classical and disinterested† education. As a direct consequence, there developed in all the Spains on both sides of the Atlantic an attitude to the young man's future which set in the proverbial phrase: "Church, sea or Royal household". That meant, a Church-cum-Law career, a merchant marine-cum-navy career or a civilian cum-military service. This tendency is still deeply rooted in the Spanish American middle class.

---

*I wrote scathingly against the abominable treatment of Indian labour in eighteenth-century textile works in Peru, as reported by two famous Spanish observers; but was told by a professor of Cuzco University that my strictures did not apply to Upper Peru where the Indian worker was well treated.

†I am not saying that the Spanish American is more disinterested than the Anglo-American, which would, in my opinion, be erroneous and unfair to the Anglo-American.

The Church made a point of protecting the native (even though many churchmen exploited him abominably). Hence the Laws of the Indies, inspired by legal principles of justice emanating from Church jurists, which, though often misunderstood or forgotten by historians, are a monument of legislation in favour both of the worker and of the peasant. Here is a contemporary Mexican voice: "The deep knowledge of the social reality, the sagacity and sense of justice of the authors of the Laws of the Indies were ignored by our nineteenth-century governments, but they were active in the Querétaro Constituent Assembly [January 1917] which drafted Article 123 in force today."* It is generally recognized today in Spanish America that "with the political independence of Mexico the situation of the working class did not change for the better. In some aspects, it changed for the worse as the colonial legislation for the protection of labour disappeared, for though it was more theoretical than practical, it did embody a system of written law."† When modern observers attribute all the evils of Spanish America to that "feudal", "colonial" time, they overlook this trough dug during the first century of independence in the actual life of the working classes. Nor were the Laws of the Indies the only source of protective labour regulations. The rules for mining promulgated by the Viceroy of Peru Don Francisco de Toledo in the second half of the sixteenth century were admired by Humboldt for their wisdom and humanity.

Similarly, the picture of a continent of nations robbed of its land by a handful of adventurers may be flattering to some minds but bears no relation to the facts. Vast estates were allotted to the victors; but there was enough land to go round and so no less vast estates were left in the hands of, or granted to, native "lords", while the peasantry was provided with common lands on the Castilian pattern, comprising individual allotments and collective lands (mostly for cattle). Hear now what General Venustiano Carranza, the organizer of the 1910-1930 revolu-

*Agustin Cue Cánovas, *op. cit.*

†Alfonso López Aparicio, *El Movimiento Obrero en México.* Quoted by Agustin Cue Cánovas in *Combate*, Mexico, Nov. 1960.

tion has to say on the matter as Acting President of Mexico in his decree of 6th January, 1915, abolishing all alienations of such communal lands:

"As the native pueblos were deprived of the lands, waters and hills which the colonial government had granted them and also the congregations and communities of their lands, and as rural property became concentrated in too few hands in the rest of the country, nothing was left to the great mass of the country-side population than to provide for its needs by letting its labour at a low price to the powerful landlords. . . ."

The matter is not merely economic. It bears directly on that issue of democracy already mentioned above. The Spanish tradition was not parliamentary but municipal. The municipal community was a landowning democracy. It reached a considerable development, particularly in Castile, where it became a kind of small republic, with its own army and flag. This was the municipal spirit which the Spaniards transferred to the New World, where it struck root so deeply that at this day in small townships near Cuzco I saw Indian *alcaldes* (mayors) dressed in "Inca" (i.e., Spanish sixteenth-century Castilian peasant) costume, solemnly carrying their silver-tipped mayoral staff.

It is in no spirit of obsolete nationalism that all this is set down. It is in order to guard against the pitfall that is awaiting us: the idea that all Spanish American troubles will cease when Spanish America is indistinguishable from the United States. The true way, on the contrary, is for Spanish America to become more Spanish American, i.e., as she acquires more being. This will not be achieved by attacking and blackening one of the three chief elements that compose her; nor by neglecting the inner political trends rooted in her own character in favour of other trends and institutions rooted in a character alien to her.

7.—UNITY: THE NATIVE ELEMENT

Furthermore, this issue of the right understanding of and respect for the Spanish roots of Spanish America is essential for the solution of her long term problem—a stable political organization—not less than of her short-term problem—a stable political defence against communism and fascism. For this solution, as we shall have to discuss it anon, rests on her achieving a considerable measure of union. Now, union in Spanish America means unity on the basis of her common Spanishness.

There may be Spanish Americans who think that no such union is necessary, and who would prefer their particular country to remain loose and unattached. For such people, there is no breach of sense in refusing to have anything to do with Spanish ways and traditions. But, as a matter of fact, one does not come across people of that opinion. The feeling that Spanish America is one in essence, no matter how divided in form, is universal. And the paradox—later to be explained—is that there are Spanish Americans who, while accepting this oneness and the consequential union which should flow from it, do not wish to be told that the source of their oneness is Spanish.

Hence "Indoamerica". But "Indoamerica" is as Spanish as Spanish America. It springs from the picturesque error which flourished in the fertile imagination of Columbus that the American continent was India; and it lumps together all the "Indios" with a disregard for their differences which is excusable in a conquistador but not in a present-day Spanish American politician displaying a string of Spanish names on his visiting card. Nor does "Indoamerica" apply to countries such as Argentina or Uruguay.

The trouble comes from the mestizo psychology. A mestizo is a Spaniard caught in the skin of an Indian, or vice-versa. The two bloods are at war.* If you assume that he is a Spaniard he will react as an Indian; if you assume he is an Indian, he will react as a Spaniard, and may even claim to have no Indian blood. The relation thus established between Spaniard and Indian through the existence of a great number of mestizos is of the utmost complexity.

This relation in its turn depends on the country and its Indians. The most tense of all may well be that observable in

---

*I have endeavoured to dramatize this situation in my novel *War in the Blood*, London, William Collins & Sons, 1957.

Mexico. Thus, though Cortés was a far greater man than Pizarro and more in sympathy with the natives, there are statues to Pizarro in Peru and none to Cortés in Mexico, while in the centre of the capital stands the monument to Cuauhtemoc. Yet, no hasty conclusion should be drawn from this fact. When I arrived in Mexico for the first time, in 1931, I was advised by my Spanish friends to avoid Cortés as a subject of my lecture. I said nothing, but when the day came for my opening lecture, I devoted it all to a full-length portrait of Cortés in all his formidable dimensions, as the father-founder of the Mexican nation. And the reception I was granted justified my surmise.*

Complex as it is, an amalgam of love and hate, pride and resentment, conquest and defeat, this attitude of the Spanish American mestizo is an obstacle in the way towards unity. Furthermore, it tends to drive outside the circle of the future union and, what is worse, of the present feelings towards it, the two non-Indian nations, Argentina and Uruguay.

It is, of course, an irrational attitude. No logic need therefore be expected from it. Thus, in some extreme cases it endeavours to attain Spanish American unity by short-circuiting Spanish culture, maintaining that the Indian must reach universality on his own wings so to speak. This is in particular the case of some of the most extreme minds in what is known as *indigenismo*. It is obvious, nevertheless, that Spanish American culture can only insert itself in the family tree of universal culture as a variety of Spanish culture or, more accurately, perhaps, through the Spanish element in it. Thus, the true way of incorporating the small minority of Indians who do not speak Spanish is to bring them into the culture of their respective countries by teaching them Spanish.† Such is, of course, the way all Spanish American nations understand the problem. I do not make any bones about adding that I believe it to be a very

---

*I hope I shall be allowed to add that my historical novel *The Heart of Jade,* which presents the Conquest of Mexico in what I believe to be honest colours fair to both sides, has now been in continuous favour in Mexico since its publication in 1942, and that the same favour has been lavished on my *Life of Cortés* published in 1941.

†And Portuguese in Brazil.

poor service to our common civilization that these Indians should be taught either the Protestant faith in Spanish or the Catholic faith in English or, worst of all, a Protestant faith in English.

8.—UNITY: THE SPANISH ELEMENT

Someone once described Spain as the land of paradoxes. Here is a case in point. A glance—an unbiased glance, though—at history is enough to show that the unity of Spanish America is rooted in its common Spanishness. Nevertheless, the more Spanish these nations are the more they feel that dispersive, fissiparous, separatist tendency which characterizes the Spaniard. The effects of this tendency on Spanish American public life are obvious. It is this innate separatism of the Spaniard, as opposed to the co-operative instinct of the Anglo-Saxon, which has given rise to the Disunited States of America south of the United States of America.

There is no contradiction in all this. The political and national disunion of the Spanish American nations is a feature common to all of them and, therefore, a feature which makes them feel one. Spanish Americans (and for that matter Spaniards) travel about in each other's countries, settle there and often share actively in the public life of their host country with little or no risk of being reminded that they are strangers. I have known a Cuban and a Venezuelan who lived in Spain and when their party at home was in power they would blossom out as minister or consul general of their countries, and when their party was out of power became civil governors of Spanish provinces.

When the Spanish monarchy fell in 1931, I happened to be in Mexico City. The day before the Foreign Secretary, Genaro Estrada, had read me the text of the message which he was to publish the next day alongside of President Hoover's on the occasion of the first celebration of the Day of the Americas. Both speeches were banished to the inner and back pages of the papers because the fall of the Spanish Monarchy made hotter news. Moreover there had been a riot in Mexico over this

Spanish event and thirty demonstrators had been wounded. They were all Mexican.

The Spanish root of Spanish American unity therefore cannot be ignored. The more so as the paradox cannot be left out of account either: this Spanish root feeds a certain amount of separatism. Both strains converge in the following incident that actually happened recently in Mexico. A Spaniard, of course not even a naturalized Mexican, was proposing to a municipal council of which he was a member that a street lamp be erected at a particularly dark corner of that small township. There was a long discussion, which the mayor closed by putting the Spaniard's motion to the vote. Everyone voted "Yes" but when it came to the Spaniard, who voted last, he uttered a firm "No". Asked for an explanation, he simply said: "I hate unanimity."

Spanishness is the solvent for the non-Spanish elements which are as different as the Italians of the Estuary, the Germans of Chile, the Chinese and Japanese of Peru, a score of different Indians; very much as Englishness is the solvent for the many elements that make up the American nationality. Once the idea has been accepted that the peoples of Spanish America can only be saved through union, any action directed against their common Spanishness must be condemned as either an error or a crime.

9. — SKIES

I was once walking along the winding, pleasant streets of a garden suburb in California when I noticed that the gardeners who were tending the flowers were all Mexican Indians (How far mestizo? Not much, anyhow). I stopped by the nearest one and, in Spanish, asked him what his nationality was. "I am a Spaniard," he answered. There and then, in mid-twentieth century, I found a living confirmation of that thrice-secular Spanish American tradition which I had underscored in my historical work, *The Fall of the Spanish American Empire*. The white Creoles in the Indies were "Spaniards"; the Spaniards were "Europeans". What that Mexican Indian gardener meant by saying "I am a Spaniard" was "I am a white Mexican".

Behind this story lies one of the strongest sociological forces acting in the Indies from 1500 to 1800. On the one hand, the earth, the Indian and the Negro drew down the white towards the roots and the soil; on the other, the Spanish Court, honours, power, and the white drew up the Indian and the Negro towards the sky of culture, well-being and civilization. The coloured woman who married or mated with a white man knew she was rising towards the sky and she felt she was rooting that white man into the American earth. This urge to become white or merely whiter was a deeper hunger than mere snobbish ambition or hankering. It was the way the earth fed herself with men, and the way men sought the light of the upper skies.

These upper skies were situated in Spain, were in fact Spain, for three centuries. With the invasion of Napoleon and the subsequent fall of Spain on the world stage, the exalted position which she had occupied as the sky of Spanish America passed to France, then to Britain, then to the United States. The habit is so old that Spanish America has remained a sky-seeking country. If the United States were to disappoint her, if she felt no longer able to say:

"*C'est aujourd'hui du nord que nous vient la lumière*"
and from the obscured North were to turn to the unknown East, whose fault would it be?

Here, a warning. Many things have happened in the world since the days of Bolívar and Ferdinand VII. The rhetoric of the wars of Independence has grown thin. Spain has become again—if not a "sky", at least a home for most Spanish Americans. They find there the source of their character, the prototype of their cities, familiar ways. They also find a dictator who reminds them of their own brands. They even find their own brands actually in the flesh. There, in Spain, is Perón. There came Trujillo to sport himself and Laureano Gómez to learn the art and science of the secret police. Spain remains for good or ill the mother country of Spanish American nations, and everything that happens in Spain today may happen in Spanish America tomorrow.

III

THE AMERICAN ASPECT

I. — GENERAL OBSERVATIONS

B E F O R E coming closer to the subject of the relations between the United States and Latin America, it is indispensable to
place the subject as a whole in a world perspective. Any views on
any international subject that do not set themselves into our contemporary scheme of things, no matter how well founded they
may be on the ideas or emotions of the persons concerned, are
bound to lead to frustration and failure. Now the scheme of
things in which we live happens to make of the United States
the key nation for the future of the world.

It must be owned that this paramount consideration is far too
often overlooked by critics of the United States; indeed, is it not
too often neglected by the United States herself? It is therefore imperative to recall the fact as forcibly as possible from
the very outset of our enquiry, and in the process, to define and
clarify it to the best of our ability. The scheme of things in which
we are living presents a number of features which must
be clearly, if briefly, sketched.

Mostly owing to the progress of applied science, the world
is rapidly evolving towards a world community, may indeed be
said to be already a community. News, views, emotions, travel
throughout the planet in less time than it took them to move
across a Greek *agora;* and men fly round the world in much less
time than Julius Caesar or indeed Napoleon took to ride across
France. Since the world is already one community, it must,
sooner or later, be governed as one commonwealth. But for a
community to become a commonwealth it must be unanimous
on a minimum of ideas about itself and the world.

This degree of unanimity is for the present unattainable because there is a Great Schism on. The evolution of the European spirit inspired on its intellectual side by Socrates, on its affective side by Christ, is challenged by a heretical sect which denies both truth and love for the sake of a theoretical construction of the society of men which men, when free, reject. This Schism is unbridgeable.

The world commonwealth can therefore be built only if either the one or the other of the political philosophies facing each other eliminates its adversary. The liberal philosophy relies on discussion, free trial and error, and spontaneous agreement. The communist philosophy relies on dogma and police force. Logically, therefore, the communist philosophy should spread by the sword—and so it does whenever it can.

Expansion by force, however, has become an impossibility owing to the devastating power of modern weapons. This circumstance has fundamentally altered the character of the political evolution of the world from a community to a commonwealth; for it has determined a movement from arms to ideas, from force to public opinion, and therefore, in an essential and inescapable way, from the communist to the liberal way of doing things. It means, therefore, that the Communist Party must henceforth reserve its genuine methods—fraud and force, power and oppression—for carefully circumscribed, local operations, while carrying on its world fight by means of the essentially liberal weapons which are arguments, ideas, discussion, conviction.

This, however, presupposes that the deterrent effect of the modern means of destruction is effective on the communist leadership. For such a thing to happen, it has been indispensable for the United States to organize the superb system of defence which she has erected out of almost nothing since the communist aggression on Korea awoke the nation to the danger. Those who remember what the armed forces of America were in 1898, or even in 1916, will no doubt feel the deepest admiration, and gratitude, for such an achievement. And this is the first of the two reasons why no view on international relations is worth expressing today that does not take into consideration the

paramount importance of the United States for the very existence and future of man and his works on earth.

Nevertheless, it is only the first, and though so weighty, not
perhaps the weightier of the two. For the very success of the
American defence system neutralizes so to speak the military,
or defence, aspect of things altogether and causes a shift of stress
from force to opinion in the factors that determine world policy.
Now this shift of stress should warm the heart of every democrat, because it means an inevitable evolution from autocracy
to democracy, since autocracy is based on force and democracy
on opinion.

It follows that the aim of the war—"Which war?" you ask.
"Is there a war on?" Of course there is. A war is a conflict of
wills. The Great Schism mentioned above generates a conflict
of wills. This conflict bears on how the world community is going
to evolve into a world commonwealth: by means of a resigned
conformity enforced from above by one party, one secret police
and one army, or through a unanimity gradually blossoming
from its roots, like the unanimous harmony of a garden. May I
now return to my line of argument? The aim of this war must
therefore be to conquer public opinion by an honest and sincere
debate on the part of the West, by every possible measure and
device on the part of the communist world.

This means that henceforth the struggle will be less and less
one of force (granted a strong defence to neutralize the adversary), more and more one of authority. That (relatively recent)
habit of describing dictatorial, tyrannical, despotic régimes as
authoritarian must be rejected as singularly unfortunate. Authority is the very opposite of force. Force is a bully that steals
obedience. Authority is given acquiescence out of the abundance of the heart. The power of the Queen of England is almost
nil. Her authority is immense. The power of Franco is immense.
His authority is nil.

Fortunately for us, the world is evolving in such a way that
its affairs are being solved more and more by authority, less and
less by force. It follows that *it is of primary importance for the*

*very survival of our civilization that the United States enjoy the
highest possible moral authority in the world.*

And that is my second point, far more weighty (I do believe)
than the first. We all, free citizens of the still free part of the
world,* owe the United States admiration and gratitude for the
magnificent achievement of her watch and defence system; but
we also owe the United States all the support it is in our power
to offer in order to uphold in the world her moral authority,
without which the cold war must be lost.

It is in this spirit that the following pages have been written.

2. — MORAL AUTHORITY SQUANDERED

It may safely be said that no country in man's history has
reached a peak of moral authority as high as that the United
States possessed at the time of the Marshall Plan. Moral
authority, not prestige. The world would be a better place if the
word *prestige* were banished from its vocabulary, and what it
represents from its thoughts and attitudes. Prestige is a form of
national vanity. It is a poor substitute for moral authority.

At the time of the Marshall Plan the United States reached an
historical summit of moral authority. As President Eisenhower
left the public stage, the moral authority of the United States
was at its lowest ebb. Let American public opinion be in no
doubt about it, misinformed though it often is on these matters.
Information is not easy. (There is the language difficulty, the
courtesy of the foreigner asked, who would hesitate to offend,
may be other similar obstacles.) The fact is that in wider and
wider circles Americans are more and more disliked and, what
is still worse, less and less respected.

The causes are many and complex, but may be classed into
three orders: spontaneous-unfair; induced-unfair; spontaneous-fair.

The first order of causes of the widespread dislike of Americans is mostly due to the darker side of human nature: ingrati-

---

*Even though, for some of us, this privilege has to be paid for with
exile.

6

tude, envy, pride. Man being what he is, this saturnine reaction
of the recipients of favour to the jovial giver can no more be
avoided than the cool, dark shadows cast by the sunlit walls on
the corners where the dank air rots and stinks. We just pass on.

The induced-unfair order of causes for dislike of the Americans is due to the ever active militancy of the Communist Party.
It has been dealt with—insofar as such an ubiquitous activity
can be—in a previous chapter. It is perfectly able, if need be, to
work on nothing as raw material, as was shown in the now forgotten campaign started by Chinese communists on the use of
bacteriological weapons in the Korean war. But, of course, it
works better on good genuine raw material. And that is why the
third order of causes is twice to be regretted.

This in its turn splits into two sub-orders; the first more
superficial and more irritating; the second, more profound and,
in the long run, far more dangerous. The first can be shortly
described as *friction*. It is composed of all the small occasions
for trouble and strife that arise in the constant rubbing against
each other of human surfaces of different texture. American
soldiers and civilians are nowadays present, settled, active, in so
many places in the world, under so many climates and civilizations that it would be a miracle if at least a good handful of
incidents did not occur every hour on the planet; and an even
more wonderful miracle if in these inevitable incidents the
Americans were always right and the natives wrong. The responsibility of the American government in endeavouring to reduce
this kind of friction to a minimum is obvious; but the subject
need not detain us any longer.

The second sub-order of spontaneous-fair criticism of the
United States is, however, far more serious. It poses the fundamental question: War, yes. But for the defence of what? When
the Marshall Plan was offered to Europe, the world was still
resonant with the answer to that question: Liberty! And our
ears still remember the sound of that word vibrating in the voice
of Roosevelt and in the voice of Churchill. That word was not
to be heard again until on 20th January, 1961, it rang over the
whole earth with the voice of Kennedy.

The nation that had led the world in her struggle for liberty had gradually become the friend and ally of every dictator in the world, every nation-breaker who had gangstered his way to power and simply laughed outright at liberty and democracy and the rest of it. Forgetting that the stress had shifted from arms to faith, from conquering to convincing, the nation that had given forth Jefferson and Lincoln embraced Franco and Tito for the sake of bases and harbours; and grew so discreet about the freedom of Eastern Europe that the world began to wonder whether Washington and London were not thinking of letting Eastern Europe go for good for the sake of "peace". Unable to rally its friends for lack of a rallying cry and a banner, the West grew disgruntled, disorientated and divided. Power-policy reappeared, hardly rejuvenated by a laborious face-lift; and the free world verbal currency was debased to such an extent that the word *peace* uttered by Khrushchev was accepted as good money, and John Foster Dulles left Madrid declaring that he and Franco had studied matters of common interest for the *free* nations of the world. Faced with such deliberate counterfeiting carried out openly by its own verbal bankers, the public opinion of the world ceased to grant them any credit. When Eisenhower left office (not without sending a cordial message of thanks to Franco "for his services to world peace") no one anywhere believed any longer in anything. Least of all in the United States.

3.—LINCOLN FORGOTTEN

Since our chief aim must be to restore the moral authority of the United States, it is now our task to endeavour to find out how and why it was lost.* The loss of moral authority came about for a complex system of reasons which may well repay a moment of attention. It originated in the Pentagon, owing to

*Having written above words that amount to describing as a trough in moral authority the period between Truman-Acheson and Kennedy's accession, I might be open to the reproach of partisanship in favour of the Democrats. Things are not quite as simple as all that; since it will be found that one of the most disastrous lines of policy—the alliance with Franco—was prepared under the Truman administration. This concrete point may have to be developed at a later stage.

the professional pressure to stress the needs of the defence apparatus. Such a stressing was, of course, not merely legitimate but indispensable. It should have been the task of the State Department and the White House to have pointed out that, since the world was nowadays governed predominantly by public opinion, the defence apparatus should be conceived in such a way as not to impair the authority of the United States or the faith of the West in its own cause.

The solution adopted was the very worst. It consisted in seeking the alliance of anyone who suited the defence apparatus no matter how injurious this alliance might be to the faith and morale of the West, and *to pretend that the new ally was all right,* i.e., to fool the people. In so doing the spokesmen of the American people forgot that Lincoln's famous utterance now rules the whole world community: "You can fool some of the people all the time, and all the people some of the time; but you cannot fool all the people all the time."

And, at this point, I must return to the more specific problem of Latin America, to which, of course, all that precedes applies. It is a moot point how far American public men, pressmen and businessmen fondly imagine that they will be believed when they say or write plausible, pleasant platitudes having only a somewhat remote relation to the facts. The general tone is too often condescending and conventional, like that of two aunts talking to each other for the benefit of small nephews and nieces listening or overhearing. Do they realize that they are speaking to one of the most sophisticated varieties of western man? Whom did Mr Holland, Undersecretary of State to Mr Dulles, think he was addressing when in Buenos Aires he drank the health of Perón dubbing him "the great Argentine, the great American"? Didn't he realize that he was ruining his own reputation and integrity before a highly intelligent public? Wasn't much that was written and said at the time when the Arbenz government was ousted by means that to this day remain both mysterious and only too clear, couched in this aunt-before-the-children style? Or, as the French love to put it: *Qui trompe-t-on ici? Anglice* who is being fooled?

Once again, let us not forget Lincoln's wise pronouncement. Let us not imagine that all this sermonizing of pleasant, plausible platitudes is going to take in everybody every time. The peoples of Iberian stock or culture to whom they are addressed know a proverb which warns: *Love means deeds, not good reasons.* How wise of President Kennedy to have uttered this very thought in his own way in the first words he addressed to Latin America: "To our sister republics south of our border, we offer a special pledge—to convert our good words into good deeds."

4.—THE ROOT OF THE TROUBLE

It cannot be denied that under this unhappy tendency to talk down to the Latin Americans there lurks a sense of superiority towards the "lesser breeds without the law". There are two Americas, and the Northern English-speaking, predominantly Protestant, gregarious, prosperous American looks down on the southern, Spanish- or Portuguese-speaking, Catholic, individualist, impecunious American not unlike the way Ulster looks down on Ireland. Underneath it all, the root cause of the trouble is the deep-lying anti-Spanish prejudice in the American *ethos*. It betrays itself again in that very adjective I have just used deliberately for the first time: *American*. The United States of *America*. There is in this young, vigorous and healthy nation a sense that the whole continent is its predestined estate, an impulse (kept alive under more modern and genteel notions) which would merely carry ever farther the expansion that turned the thirteen States into the owner of the continent from the Atlantic to the Pacific and from the Great Lakes to the Gulf. Now all this expansion, or most of it, ran over lands of the Crown of Spain. It was hard for the Northerner to suppress his feeling that the expansion of "America" would know no other limits than those of America. Those Spaniards? Well, what about them? What on earth are they there for, squatting in our estate? This was not reason. It was life, manifest destiny.

5. — THE MONROE DOCTRINE

Manifest destiny. The initials were the same as those of the
Monroe Doctrine. And when all is said and done, the Monroe
Doctrine, by its mere unilateralism, amounted to a degradation
of the Latin American countries to the status of protectorates.
Much water has flowed over the rivers of both Americas since
1823, but the impulses and attitudes which expressed themselves in the Monroe Doctrine remain very much alive.

I remember that in the days when the spirited young men of
the State Department had not got to screen the fire of their eyes
in order not to dazzle the young men of the U.N. Secretariat,
I was asked, at question time at a banquet-cum-speech, what I
thought of the Monroe Doctrine. My answer was: "I only know
two things about the Monroe Doctrine: one is that no American
I have met knows what it is; the other is that no American I
have met will consent to its being tampered with. That being so,
I conclude that the Monroe Doctrine is not a doctrine but a
dogma, for such are the two features by which you can tell a
dogma. But when I look closer into it, I find that it is not one
dogma but two, to wit: the dogma of the infallibility of the
American President and the dogma of the immaculate conception of American foreign policy."

Years have gone by, and the American people have matured
in matters of foreign policy with a speed unequalled elsewhere.
And yet, I suspect that though one hears less about the Monroe
Doctrine than in the days of old, the two dogmas have kept their
vigorous hold on the hearts of the people of the United States.
There is in the American public a touching disposition to spontaneous acquiescence in what happens to be at the time the
official line, a faith in the infallibility of the President and a
staunch belief in the immaculate conception of the State
Department's policy; both possibly animated by an even deeper
degree of faith in the manifest destiny of the United States of
America to become as big as her name. And it will be one of our
tasks to try to find out how far this blustering spirit is still work-

ing under the internationally more respectable forms of Pan-american-led or other American-led institutions.

6.—LATIN AMERICA?

It is, for instance, disappointing to find that even this very year books are being published in the United States based on the crudest misconceptions about the viceregal days in Spanish America, which they insist on describing as "colonial" against all historical evidence. I shall have to refer to some of these misconceptions in the coming pages when discussing the subject to which they refer.* This aspect of the question is serious, for it means that public opinion in the U.S.A. is denied the possibility of adequately understanding the historical and psychological roots of the problem, since these roots are, of course, deeply embedded in Spain.

The field is so vast that the task can be begun almost anywhere. For instance by a discussion on the very name of the object of our study. I have described it as Spanish America. It is generally known in the United States, Britain, France and Italy—*but not in other European nations*—as Latin America. One meets with both names in Spanish America itself. Why these differences in the label?

The origin must be found in a psychological interest or stand common to the United States, Britain, France and Italy but not shared by Germany or Scandinavia. History provides the answer. Britain and France, followed by the United States, have been the chief adversaries of Spain in the New World. "Latin" instead of "Spanish" symbolizes the cultural tail of that once

---

*May I state here that the section "The Colonial Heritage", pp. 12-15 of the pamphlet *The U.S. and Latin Americas* by W. S. Woytinsky, published by *The New Leader* in 1960, later by the Tamiment Institute, is a hotchpotch of ignorant and prejudiced statements which bid fair to contain more errors than words. This is the more remarkable for the fact that, on his own ground, as an economist, the author is a reliable and competent guide to whom I owe a number of facts and figures adduced in this essay.

war-like comet. The name is used as a means to expel Spain culturally from the continent from which she had been expelled politically. Such an interest is shared by Italy on account of her own demographic invasion of South America. It means nothing to Germany or to Sweden.

I shall not waste time in the argument that "Latin" is meant to include Haiti, which is French-speaking, since, among other reasons, such an argument would lead to including in Latin America the French-speaking regions of Canada.

Central European nations speak of *Iberian America*, which is correct. My reasons for preferring Spanish America are three (at any rate when writing in English, for the first reason does not apply to the Spanish language at all): this first is that Iberian America is longer and clumsier. The second is that while *Iberia* and *Spain* are synonymous since both mean the whole peninsula, *Iberian* describes but one of the many human components of the Spanish people; and the third is that, without any prejudice whatsoever as to the independence and separate existence of the nation called Portugal, the Portuguese are as Spanish as the other Spaniards; so that one can describe Portugal as part of Spain and therefore Brazil as part of Spanish America, without being lunatic enough to wish to absorb Portugal into present-day political "Spain" any more than Brazil into Argentina.*

*The trouble here comes from the fact that with Portugal's final separation from the rest of Spain in the seventeenth century, the word *Spain* remained attached to the biggest of the two portions, into which the Peninsula was split. During the negotiations for an armistice between France and Portugal at Utrecht in 1712, the Portuguese claimed to refer to the kingdom of Spain as "Castille". This was contested by the French, but the foreign minister Torcy explained nevertheless to the French plenipotentiaries that the Portuguese claim was based on the fact that it was *"un ancien usage chez eux fondé sur ce qu'ils regardent le Portugal comme une partie des Espagnes et qu'ils ne veulent pas convenir que le Roy d'Espagne soit Roy de tout ce continent"*. A parallel with England will illustrate the verbal difficulty. All over Europe, it is usual to speak of *England* meaning *Great Britain*. But England means in fact what remains when you slice off Wales and Scotland. In Spain, the reverse is the case. Spain is generally used for "Spain minus Portugal" and there are even Catalans and

7. — WIVES AND POTTERY

As an example of what is here meant and of its direct relevancy to the subject of this book, I reproduce below a page I wrote elsewhere:

I have before me a copy of a well-known and widely-read American magazine; no merely commercial paper, but one purporting to be organized for the diffusion of knowledge. It carries an article on Panama. After a preface on the "looting" of gold by the Spaniards, and on how "for years the wealth of the stricken country of the Incas poured across the Isthmus over the gold road from Old Panama to Portobello on its way to Spain", we come to this sub-title: "GOLD DOOMED RICH NATIVE COUNTRY." "The very riches of the natives brought about their early doom," we are told. Then we are introduced to Parita, a chief of this "rich" civilization which was "doomed" because of its wealth. The Spanish gold-looter, Espinosa, on returning, presumably for more loot, found that Parita had died. "Breaking into the house where his body lay in state, the Spaniards obtained one of the richest hauls of loot ever recovered. Lashed to the house posts by cords tied around their throats were twenty Indian captives who had been destined to be buried alive with the great chieftain." So, that was the "rich" civilization which was "gold-doomed". But let us read on. "The burial rites of these Indians were unusually elaborate"; please note the word *elaborate*. "After the death of an important chief, funeral ceremonies lasted for two days. During this period his wives and household attendants were prepared for burial with him." Then comes a sub-title: "WIVES AND SERVANTS BURIED ALIVE."

Basques who are now using it for "Spain minus Portugal minus Catalonia, minus the Basque country"; but there is no name for that lump that remains; in the matter of the language the situation is even more confused. There is really no adequate name for "the language of Cervantes". "Spanish" is not accurate, for Catalan, Gallegan and even Basque and Portuguese are as much "Spanish" as it is. "Castilian" is not accurate either for it was born in Northern Castile and the Basque country, and it is the only language of countries as un-Castilian as Aragon. However, I do not propose to go against the established tradition, and I have accepted "Latin America" for this work.

Then a description of how this was done, and how "sometimes
as many as fifty individuals and a fortune were thus buried with
an important chief"; then examples of a tomb found with twenty-
one, and another one with thirty-two women buried alive; and,
immediately after, this: "Evidence of the high state of their
culture is some of the most beautiful pottery produced in the
New World."

It was necessary to go into some detail and to quote generously (I am speaking of quantity), for this article, which pur-
ports to be scientific, is a good example of the misinterpretation
and misrepresentation of Spanish history from which our whole
West is suffering. The stress on gold and on looting, which every
good historian of our day rejects as unscientific, remains, nevertheless, as active as ever; despite the admirable work of American scholars such as Professor Hamilton, who have reduced to
their relatively modest proportions the flow of gold and silver
into Spain; and the evident fact that Latin America was never
more prosperous and rich, never had more style and colour,
than under the Spanish sway; the old, outworn, unscientific
image of a New World bled white by Spanish greed is still
trotted out as ever; the bias backs the Indian even when afflicted
by such dreadful social errors as that of burying alive his wives
and servants or of eating his war prisoners. Such rites are described as "elaborate". I shudder to think of the epithets they
would elicit were they Spanish, and not Indian, rites. The gold-
looting Spaniard is splashed large over the page; but the
Christianizing Spaniard who put a stop to the burying of wives
alive and to the eating of war prisoners does not figure in the
story at all. And then there is that curious twist: after a cold,
objective, and uncondemned description of tombs full of victims
buried alive, this sudden and surprising estimate of values:
"Evidence of the high state of their culture is some of the most
beautiful pottery produced in the New World."

So, high culture means beautiful pottery and burying your
wife alive when you die. Is that it? Are we to understand that
culture means an advanced state of man's control over matter,
even when his attitude towards the things of the spirit is appal-

ling? For if that is what culture means, the West has no longer any answer to the communist conception of life, in the name of which men are tortured and shot as a holocaust to the Five Year Plan. It is therefore vital, even at the risk of being misunderstood, to bring out into the open that tendency to carry efficiency and effectiveness to the point of ruthlessness which lurks at times behind the American way of life. This American way of life is not a set and crystallized affair. It is still in the making, like all things truly alive; and we must not wonder if, along with the finest liberal, spiritual and creative trends, it also carries in its mighty flow other trends of a less generous and fertile character. For good or ill, the centre of gravity of the world is now shifting to the West. The New Atlantis, the citadel formed by the nations on the shores of the Atlantic, is fast becoming the centre of the future world. No one can deny to the United States the leading share in this phase of human history. But no one can deny either that, after the Anglo-Saxon, the Hispanic element is bound to be the strongest in it. How is this Hispanic factor likely to play on the rich and complex instrument of American life? Which of the trends in it is the Hispanic element more likely to stimulate, to echo, to reinforce?

The answer is not in doubt: the human. That means neither the humane nor the humanistic. For instance: it means that the Spaniard is more interested in wives than in pottery, but it does not necessarily mean that he will always treat his wife well, or be as obedient to her as the average American is to his own wife and to the wives of his friends. What it does mean is that he will treat her as a human being; and therefore, with love, passion, deference, hate, contempt, admiration, companionship, fun, awe, kindness, vindictiveness, generosity, meanness, humility or pride—but never with that scientific, meticulous, condescending, distant care with which the archaeologist treats antique pottery.

8. — SPANISH CULTURE IN THE U.S.A.

This way of distorting the history of Spain in the United

States acts as a powerful brake on any movement for a better mutual understanding between the two Americas and should be corrected if the moral health of the continent is to reach the level it needs to attain before it can conquer the communist (and the fascist) menaces. The small band of American historians, teachers and specialists in charge of Spanish culture in the United States who have been working in this field with so much devotion and understanding must be able to feel that they are contributing not merely to true knowledge but to the preservation of freedom in the New World and therefore in the Old World. The country of Unamuno, Ortega, Picasso, Casals, Segovia, Lorca must no longer be looked down upon as one whose culture does not matter, and whose language, accordingly, need not be taught, as was the belief of that young Inspector of Education in Wisconsin who in six months managed to close down all Spanish classes in his zone. True, Spanish is perhaps the language which attracts the highest number of students in the United States; but this is far too often due to positive and practical reasons, for Latin America is considered rather as a market, and at most a political problem, than as a culture. In the publishers' world, for instance, the mere fact that the author is a Frenchman will double the chances of his manuscript being accepted; the mere fact that he is a Spaniard will reduce them by half; so that, the intrinsic value of the script being the same, the Frenchman starts with a fourfold advantage over the Spaniard.

Curiously enough, this intellectual disdain towards Spanish culture is relatively recent, indeed a matter of the twentieth century.* The interest for things Spanish and the knowledge of Spanish books in the United States was considerable in the seventeenth, eighteenth and even nineteenth centuries, and this high esteem for Spanish culture did not stop at literature but covered also scientific work which was deservedly praised by American scientists. This attitude became almost traditional thanks to a chain of illustrious American names such as

The Spanish Background of American Literature by Stanley T. Williams, Yale University Press, 1955.

Washington Irving, Ticknor, Prescott, Longfellow, Lovell, Howells; yet, as time went by, and as American life itself grew wider, hispanism became perhaps more and more of a special feature in the general landscape, so that in the days of Waldo Frank, Hemingway and Thornton Wilder, despite their penetrating sympathy, interest in Spain so far as the general public and even the general *élite* is concerned, is at a low ebb. This general public and *élite* are willing to be interested in Spanish and Latin American ways and life as objects of study, just as one is interested in pottery or coins; they are not, however, ready to admit Spanish and Latin American life as subjects and initiators of culture and civilization on an equal footing with that of the United States and of the rest of Europe.

9. — WHY NEGLECTED ?

The reasons may be many and complex; and only a sketchy analysis will here be attempted. There is at the root of it all a tradition of Protestant enmity, often in the old days clouded with ignorance and arrogance, which saw the Spanish world as a dark dungeon vibrating with the shrieks of the victims of the Inquisition. This tradition merges with one of sea-freebooters, pirates and corsairs who found it profitable both for body and soul to pry on Spanish gold and goods, thus gaining a fortune if they came out alive and a stool in Calvin's Heaven if they came out dead. In the wake of this struggle came the several acquisitions, some of them peaceful, others less so, of the immense territories which belonged to the Crown of Spain in 1800 and are today part of the United States; then the Mexican war with the huge annexation of Mexican territory it entailed; then the Cuban war with the annexation of Puerto Rico, then the big-stick adventures in Panama, Mexico, Nicaragua, Santo Domingo, etc. This era of struggle and spirited expansion necessitated as a psychological adjunct a systematic denigration of the adversary. A good deal of the mud has stuck.

Then there is the strong technological and economic bias of our present age, which inevitably tends to mechanize human life and reduce human liberty, to stress security, prosperity and conformity against freedom, carefree improvidence and originality. The North stands thus for an ideal of society which goes against the grain of the South, and as this difference is bound to manifest itself in a difference of standard of living to the advantage of the North, a certain element of disdain is bound to step in.

Finally, if we transfer what proceeds from the individual-in-society to the nation-in-history, we find that the very trends of her genius were bound to make of the United States a nation rapidly rising to the unequalled position she occupies today as the chief guardian and banner of the West; while Spain cuts the figure of a nobleman who, having owned vast estates, has gradually allowed them to be grabbed away, and now sits silent in his leaky and windy house.

It is a pity. For the future of America, this time I mean the whole continent, demands a cordial collaboration and mutual understanding between the United States, Latin America, Britain and Spain. (I should also like to add France, not merely because of French Canada and Haiti, but also because from France emanates the strongest European influence on the continent, after that of Britain in the North and of Spain in the South.) No such cordial collaboration can thrive while obsolete prejudices encumber the attitude of the North towards the South . . . and of the South towards the North. But some of us may perhaps be allowed to recall here that liberal-minded Spaniards have twice shown their capacity to overcome national prejudices (which in their case might have been justified by such symbolical names as Gibraltar, Santiago and Cavite) and come out openly on the side of Britain and the United States in 1914-18 and in 1939-45; and that we are still on their side in 1962 even though since 1953 they have become the allies of the Spanish dictator and one-time ally of Hitler. We may therefore be allowed to hope that the following pages will be read with trust and benevolence by American readers.

10. — THE TENSION BETWEEN NORTH AND SOUTH

Search as you may, you will not be able to find on the whole earth a continent in which tensions are so simple and direct as in America. Elsewhere the bewildering variety of national characters and of geographic situations has been knotted up by centuries of history into the most complicated patterns. In America, apart from Canada (a ship still British moored in New World waters), there is but one tension: the "Anglic" North versus the Hispanic South.

Curiously enough, it is a tension somehow reminiscent of that which on the eve of the discovery of America polarized the energies of Spain towards Islamic Africa. Even to the extent that the receding male-God-worshipping Muslims were then being threatened by a pent-up wave of Christians who were all devout worshippers of the Holy Virgin. For there is probably some substance in the claim that the United States is a matriarchate; while Latin America is a father-governed culture and civilization. To the query, "How is it then that it is the North that takes the initiative?", the answer would be "Precisely".

Everything drives Anglic America towards Hispanic America. Historical memories, geographical neighbourhood, investments for finance, activity for commerce, harbours, islands and canals for strategy, living contrasts for tourism, search for beauty and the picturesque, for a change from weariness and the drab utilitarian life of the prosperous, desire to help and uplift others for the idealist, easy money and even power for the "realist", and what not other impulses all rolled into one feeling of go-getting.

The question that arises at this point is not how to resolve or even how to reduce this tension; or how to stem this rush of energy southward. The question is one of finality. Where do we want to go? Do we want America to become a huge United States from the Hudson Bay to Cape Horn, in the southern part of which people will be plunged into a chaos of cultures, talking the kind of English-Spanish one hears in New Mexico and is beginning to hear in Puerto Rico? Or do we want America to be a continent in which a rich banker-manufacturer-shipper becomes richer and richer by drawing as much profit as he can from his southern neighbours without actually impoverishing them to the point of destroying his own markets? Or do we want America to become a happy family of nations belonging to two definitely different varieties of the same European civilization, peacefully developing together their resources by mutual help asked and given on the basis of commonsense and freedom?

We shall assume that the path chosen is the third. For then, the tension between Anglic North and Hispanic South, which is today at its most dangerous, will become a fertile force both for the material and for the moral future of the whole continent.

II. — THE MONSTER-MACHINE

Meanwhile, there can be no doubt about the overwhelming nature of the hold of the North over the South. The power of the North is so huge compared to that of the South that, like a machine or a monster, it paralyses and devours the nearly defenceless South, so that all that remains free and independent there might be said to owe its freedom and independence less to its own exertions than to the moderation and wisdom of the North.

The machine grows with its own exertions. The equipment sold and installed demands spare parts and replacements; the loans lead to partnership then to ownership of trade firms; trade brings in reserves in the local currency which it is best to employ locally in the purchase of capital goods or in a lateral extension of trade activities. Publicity keeps on their feet newspapers that might have fallen by the wayside, which leads to part-owning them, then to owning them entirely. Public opinion is thus shaped and conditioned; local men are given salaries, hopes, careers; a flavour and a direction is imparted to public opinion. And none of this is done by "the United States". It is done by Mr American Citizen, or by Private Enterprise Unlimited. Only, should anything go wrong, European competition, local cussedness, a mistake, a scandal due to a disappointed would-be corruptee or a swindled American would-be corrupter, the possibility of a new railway line or steel furnace or hydraulic dam going to another industrial power, why, even a local revolution threatening seriously to injure the locally acting agency of Private Enterprise Unlimited, the Southern Government is sure to be called to order by that most powerful man in the nation it is supposed to rule—the Ambassador of the United States.

Now, the attitude of this exalted personage (surely not radically different from that of the State Department) has been thus described by an American observer:

Many U.S. representatives in Latin America believe that a country's pro-United States attitude must be expressed by the abstention of its government from intervention in economic affairs, its reliance on private initiative, and its hospitality toward foreign investment. If, on the other hand, a government decides to reserve exploration of oilfields to itself or relies on public regional development programs, these are manifestations of its anti-American tendencies, perhaps of pro-Communist orientation.

It is difficult to understand this reasoning. This country is not properly concerned with public or private ownership of industries in Great Britain, Germany, France and Japan and is not in the least interested in the ways in which Brazil, Mexico or Chile solve this problem. As far as the exploitation of oilfields and mines is concerned, the U.S. Government may feel its obligation to defend the interests of its citizens if they are subjected to discriminatory treatment or threatened with arbitrary expropriation of their property. Except for such a situation, it has no reason to prefer any particular form of enterprises in respective economic sectors in foreign countries. Certainly exploitation of Brazilian oil reserves by a Dutch or British corporation presents no advantage to the United States over their exploitation by an autonomous public agency. The United States could oppose a national monopoly of oil exploitation in a foreign country only if it were

7

interested in the penetration of its private capital into this field. But from the point of view of national interest, the United States gains nothing either from outflow of capital or its investment in this particular industry.

The same reasoning should be applied to public projects of regional development. Those who dislike expansion of the economic responsibilities of the Government in this country are inclined to dislike similar projects abroad. But this should be a question of personal opinion rather than a matter of foreign policy.

The attitude of U.S. representatives in Latin America on such problems as public or private ownership of industrial plants and public or private exploitation of mineral resources can be described as an attempt to export to Latin America slogans which have been rejected by our allies in Europe and are an apple of discord in U.S. internal politics. Injection of these issues into our policy in Latin America does not strengthen the prestige of this country among governments and intellectuals in these nations.*

12.—THE STRANGLEHOLD

The outcome of this situation is complex, like most economic facts, and no rash conclusions should be risked. Nevertheless, it would be surprising if it were, on balance, favourable to the South, at any rate on the material side. Nearly every Latin American country exports more than it imports. It is paying out of its substance. Whom and for what? "Whom" is easily answered. The share of the United States in the exports of Latin American countries in 1956 varied from 94.8% for Panama, 74.1% for Guatemala, 72.9% for Mexico, 71% for Colombia, 64.7% for Cuba, 59.5% for Ecuador and 55% for Bolivia to 18.1% for Paraguay, 12.5% for Argentina and 11.6% for Uruguay, these three countries being the only ones whose percentage was lower than 34.

The U.S. and Latin America's Economy by W. S. Woytinsky, New York, 1958, pp. 50-51. I owe to this pamphlet and to Professor Perroux' book *L'Europe sans Rivages* most of the figures in these pages.

For what? Remitted corporate profits in 1955 from Latin America to the United States amounted to $680 million, an estimated net return of 14% on the equity capital. Furthermore, in the same year the book value of Private Enterprise Unlimited investments in Latin America increased by one billion dollars, including only $148 million of her U.S. money. Therefore the difference, i.e., $852 million must be considered as capital gains of U.S. stockholders, bringing their total gains up to at least 30% of their capital invested. No wonder that the American economist from whom I borrow these facts comments: "The U.S. Department of Commerce emphasizes that American capital accounted for 30% of the exports of Latin American nations in 1955. It is an open question, however, whether this speaks well for our investments in the area. Production for export is a typical operation of foreign capital in colonies and has never been popular with the indigenous populations."*

If we now consider the *net* amount of foreign capital invested in Latin America in 1945-52 we find it barely amounts to 3% of the total investments of the Latin American countries concerned; and, what is worse, that this net new invested capital turns out to be lower than, indeed as little as 24% of the remittances of interest and other capital services of the invested capital. Here are the figures:

Year	Incoming capital in millions of dollars	Outgoing capital in millions of dollars	Outgoing Remittances for interest, etc.
1945	333	88	543
1951	688	142	875
1952	432	150	682

During the period 1950-53 the net investments from U.S.A. and the Inter-American Bank of Development (B.I.D.) reached a yearly average of $422 million; while the financial charges of the said capital amounted to a yearly average of $631 million. Therefore, it is in fact Latin America that is exporting capital to the U.S.A.; and as this export is not due to any increase in Latin American savings the effect is one of decapitalization of Latin America.

Out of the $422 million yearly average invested in Latin

*Woytinsky, *loc. cit.*, p. 32.

America in 1950-53, only about $80 million yearly were public investments (B.I.D. and Eximbank), i.e., 3% of the public investments of the Latin American nations concerned. (In the days when such investment was led by the London market, this percentage used to be 20.)

The average gain of direct private U.S.A. investment in Latin America was 21% in 1948, 20.5% in 1951. (In the oil industry, the yield from capital was the highest: throughout 1948-51, 40.3%.) Therefore, out of a total investment of $6,000 million (which was the figure for 1953), the yield for U.S.A. was $1,200 million, and for the whole period 1948-53, this total profit on capital amounted to $6,000 million.

The total value of foreign private capital investments in Latin America after the Second World War was for more than 60% due to reinvestments of profits, and only one third of new capital.

There are, however, other equally competent opinions which differ from this view. "The amount of annual remittances," the argument would run, "must be compared to the total investment in the country and not to the movement, purely coincidental, of new capital funds into the countries concerned. It would seem obvious—although many Latin Americans fail to see it—that the annual remittance on a capital investment (book value of $6.6 billion) would have no relation to new increments of capital coming in annually from abroad. One is an income factor and the other a capital factor."

The figures supplied by the Economic Commission for Latin America on the basis of date from Survey of Current Business, U.S. Department of Commerce, March 1961, are:

	1955	1956	1957	1958	1959
	(in millions of dollars)				
Movements of capital from U.S.A. to Latin America	357	915	1563	932	608
Remittances of interest and other charges from Latin America to U.S.A.	780	893	986	730	697

The growing dependence of Latin America on the United States is illustrated by the fact that the share of the United

States in the foreign trade of the whole region passed from 33%
to 55% for exports and 33% to 52% for imports between 1938
and 1952. But this dependence is made far closer for most of
the countries for a twofold reason: for most Latin American
countries the proportion of their foreign trade to their national
income is much higher than is the case for other more developed countries; and most of them also are dependent on one
or two products, such as bananas (Honduras), coffee (Colombia, Brazil), copper (Chile), oil (Venezuela), tin (Bolivia), the
trade in which, moreover, in a number of cases, is controlled by
American houses. The situation thus developed is sometimes
considered by the public opinion of the nations concerned as a
stranglehold.

13.—OIL

The phrase "to pour oil on troubled waters" does not apply
to the relations between the United States and Latin America.
Oil, usually a lubricant, is a constant cause of friction between
North and South. And yet, the North (both State and private
citizenry and enterprise) might have learnt not a little from the
experience of Mexico.

A case again in which the old-régime Spanish legislation
proved wiser than post-independence trends: for in viceregal
days oil deposits belonged to the Crown, i.e., the soil might be
privately owned but not the subsoil; while the Mining Code
adopted in Mexico in 1884, following the French Civil Code,
reversed the principle and allowed private ownership of the subsoil. Whence much trouble was to flow.

The first years of the century are full of noise, fire, thunder,
blood, and now and then a political scandal in Washington, such
as, for instance, the Teapot Dome affair of unsavoury memory—
all caused by private oil interests. In 1921 Mexico was producing 193 million barrels of oil. By 1932, production had fallen
to 32 million, owing to changes in the policy of the foreign
companies which controlled production and export. Between
1901 and 1937, 1,866 million barrels had been extracted from

the Mexican soil and sold at 3.60 dollars a barrel with but little benefit to the country beyond the poor salaries paid to the workers. White Guards, actual armies paid by the Oil Companies, fought against the Mexican army from 1914 to 1920 to keep the rich oil lands out of the jurisdiction of the government.

The 1917 constitution, however, explicitly declared oil to be a national asset, thus returning to the Spanish legal principle. The companies (El Aguila [British] and Huasteca [American] being the most important) reacted vigorously; and the United States was requested by them to declare war. Wilson did not listen. In 1925 a bill on oil is submitted to Parliament in Mexico; and a strong world-wide campaign of vilification of Mexico follows. It seems that war would then have been actually declared by the U.S.A. but for a timely intervention from President Calles directly to President Coolidge over the head of Secretary of State Kellogg. President Calles' revelations were of such a nature that the American Ambassador, Sheffield, had to be replaced. The new man, Monroe, was of a quieter disposition.

In 1933, Petro-Mex (Petróleo Mexicano) was founded as a State enterprise. The Mexican government was not pleased with the way things were going. Natural gas, for instance, was allowed to escape—a loss Mexican technicians put at $150 million; the tax situation was chaotic and ruinous for the State; the Huasteca Company had not built the gas pipeline to Mexico City provided for in its concession. Relations between the companies and their workers went from bad to worse.

Each company (twenty of them) dealt with a union organized by its own workers, until 1936, when the oil workers of all of them joined in a single union. A single collective contract had to be negotiated according to Mexican Labour laws. The Workers Union put forward a draft which was rejected by the companies (November 1936). The government stepped in as an honest broker, but by April 1937 the new parley had failed and the workers went on strike. The country was brought to a nearly total standstill.

The government advised the workers to appeal to the Labour

Court, considering the issue as an "economic conflict". This, according to Mexican law, entails an investigation of the facts towards a solution by conciliation and arbitration. Three technicians were appointed to report (one of them an engineer, Montezuma by name). Their report was a thoroughgoing document which threw up somewhat startling results:

(*a*) The oil companies operating in Mexico were subsidiaries of big oil entities domiciled abroad.

(*b*) These companies had been concealing profits with a view to tax evasion, by means of skilful accountancy and manipulation of prices.

(*c*) The companies were able, without endangering their financial position, to increase their outlay in salaries and other labour benefits by about 26 million Mexican pesos. (The workers' demands would have amounted to 90 million.)

(*d*) The yearly profit of the companies during the previous three years had been $56 million.

(*e*) The companies had devoted no attention to welfare or social progress of any kind. The housing of the foreign personnel was of the best; that of the workers miserable, and the malaria mosquito was omnipresent. The oil port, Tampico, exported rivers of gold but had almost no water supply.

The companies protested. The President (General Lázaro Cúrdenas) called a meeting of the twenty managers and the three experts in his own study, heard both sides and told the managers that the experts were right. On 18th December, 1937, the Conciliation and Arbitration Committee gave its award, in conformity with the experts. The companies would have to increase their expenditure on labour by 26 million pesos, a figure far closer to their own offer (14 million) than to the workers' demand (90 million). They, nevertheless, appealed to the Supreme Court, while withdrawing their funds from Mexico, and sending their railway oil tanks to the U.S.A. and their tankers to foreign ports. On 1st March, 1938, the Supreme Court confirmed the award of the Conciliation Committee. The companies refused to comply. President Cárdenas tried yet another meeting with the executives. All he got was an offer of 22,400,000 pesos;

just 3,600,000 pesos less than the figure laid down by the law
of the land. The workers gave notice of a strike for 8th March,
1938. It began in the morning. At 8 p.m. President Cárdenas
announced by radio that the twenty companies were expropriated. Hardly had he left the microphone than an emissary from
the companies arrived offering the whole 26 million.

It was too late. Expropriation it was to be. But Mexico was
left without technicians, means of transport, turnover money and
international sales machinery. To make matters worse, there
were not a few workers simple enough to imagine that now the
oil belonged to them, and a good deal of trouble of this kind
had to be met. The nation had to improvise everything. At
first, there was not enough oil for the country; later there was
too much, since there were no contracts for export and no
tankers. In the end, the crisis was overcome and exports flowed
regularly.

The next hurdle was compensation for the expropriated
owners. F. D. Roosevelt had taken expropriation with calm and
wisdom, but, of course, wanted fair compensation. To which
Mexico was ready. The companies began by asking $2,000
million, then $450 million. In the end, they agreed on $115
million, plus nearly $50 million which one of them (British)
managed to extract as interest from a more amenable administration. All was paid.

How did it work? Private production which had reached 193
million barrels in 1921 had fallen to 32 million in 1932 and
recovered to 47 million in 1937. In 1957 public production was
at 97 million barrels. Gasoline rose from 8,000 barrels a day in
1938 to 62,000 in 1958. The Mexicans have discovered 96 new
oil deposits in those twenty years. In 1938 oil reserves stood at
835 million barrels. In 1958 they stood at 3,300 million. The
length of pipelines was 1,500 kms in 1938; 6,700 kms in
1958. Three modern refineries have been built, and one of the
five old ones left over from the private enterprise régime, that
in Acapulco, has been enlarged to produce 100,000 instead of
15,000 barrels. Mexico owns 19 tankers. Investments add up to
$10 million of American money on loan and 6,800 million pesos

of Mexican money, an average of $50 million yearly in the last six years. A considerable programme of housing and welfare has been carried out.

To sum up. Private Enterprise has been shown wanting; and State Enterprise triumphant. Let us not be dogmatic. We affirm this failure of Private Enterprise Unlimited and this success of State Enterprise in the concrete case of Mexican oil in 1938-60. And we do not generalize nor draw conclusions from it except on a number of points equally concrete.

The first is that it was to the honour of F. D. Roosevelt that he did not react as Coolidge, Harding or Theodore Roosevelt might have done. He saw what was just and acted accordingly, like a President of the United States and not of Private Enterprise Unlimited.

The second is that if at the time Mexico had been led by a lesser man than Lázaro Cárdenas, the outcome of the struggle might have been disastrous. It is not necessary to agree with everything General Cárdenas does—I disagree with him on nearly everything he does nowadays—in order to realize that he had the courage and the imagination required at the time for the decision he took. And who could deny that had he been less staunch, had he yielded, compromised, bowed before the arrogant stand of the companies, an anti-American wave of mighty dimensions might have overpowered Mexico, and the world war might well have been a different story? By his stand in 1938, General Cárdenas may well have saved Mexico from that communism of which he seems to have since become too close a friend.

Finally, this story should be well noted by the State Department officials, Senators and Congressmen of the United States who only too often align themselves behind Private Enterprise Unlimited in all that concerns Latin America. The recent history of negotiations between American oil interests, Banks and the national Oil Agencies of Brazil, Argentina, Chile and Venezuela (particularly under Pérez Jiménez) has by no means increased the popularity or the moral authority of the United States in Latin America.

A distinguished American expert may here be quoted.

In much of Latin America, one of the recurring irritations centers on the emphasis on the role of U.S. business. To couch U.S. foreign policy primarily in terms of promoting U.S. business interests is as sure a way of losing friends and alienating people south of the border as could be devised. The question is not whether big business can and should play an effective role in development. In Latin America, big business is the symbol of exploitation for leftists and nationalist leaders, and this symbol has considerable reality behind it in any review of the last half-century. Furthermore, in many parts of Latin America big business is mainly foreign-owned business. The issue is not one of discouraging business from moving to Latin America, but to encourage business leaders to face up to the political and social realities of Latin America and to show foresight in adapting their plans and operations to them, rather than to depend on U.S. influence in solving their local problems. A foreign policy must represent an interaction between sovereign states, not merely a projection of the desires of one country or of some segments within it. If the United States is not strong enough politically and economically to place its national foreign policy above the pressures of particular business interests, then it is perilously close to forfeiting its right to be called a nation.

Nor is this pure theory. Here is, quoted by another distinguished American expert, what the Mexicans think of American Enterprise in Mexico:

(1) Foreign investments, especially those establishing subsidiaries of large U.S. corporations, attempt to obtain absolute control of the market and eliminate competition. (2) In addition to displacing Mexican firms, foreign-controlled firms do not always employ Mexican raw materials or semi-elaborated products—thereby retarding the development of local industry and the local market. (3) When foreign-owned or controlled companies produce raw materials or semimanu-

factured goods, they tend to exert a monopoly over the Mexican industries depending upon these products. (4) A great deal of the wealth produced with the aid of foreign investment leaves Mexico. According to the report of the Bank of Mexico, the earnings on foreign investments from 1939 to 1955 amounted to $813.7 million. During the same period $790.9 million were sent out of Mexico in the form of profits, patent fees, interest, and royalties.

This American author points out the advantages accruing to Mexico, which the Mexicans forget. They are certain and valuable but far too expensive for healthy development.*

14.—FORCED DEVALUATIONS

There comes a moment in the course of an enquiry such as this when the facts (or alleged facts) go into "obscuration", at any rate for an observer without access to the arcana of State and big enterprise administration. All the private observer can do is to report not what happens—for he does not in fact know it—but what he is told by persons whom he considers reliable and responsible. To the best of my knowledge, it is widely believed in Latin America that when powerful American houses acquire control over a particular line of trade predominant in the country concerned, they sometimes bring to bear the overwhelming influence thus acquired in order to extort currency-devaluation from the unwilling government; which at once raises the local value of their merchandise (be it coffee, tin, sugar or bananas) and places them in a position of privilege to extend their economic control to other local lines of production.

This criticism is not one which a visitor in Latin America can easily refute however strong his desire may be to keep an

---

*The general outline of the story is summed up from Jesus Silva Herzog, *Mexico y su Petroleo*, Universidad de Buenos Aires, 1959. The quotations are from Professor Richard N. Adams's Essay on Guatemala and from Banco de Mexico (1956) translated and quoted by Professor Oscar Lewis in his essay on Mexico in *Social Change in Latin America Today*.

even balance and to be fair to the United States. It is a serious complaint, if founded. It has been asserted that the suicide of Getulio Vargas during his second term as President of Brazil was due to American pressure on him to devalue the cruzeiro (1954). This may or may not be so; but it is vital for the United States to realize that the belief in such a dramatic event is seriously held by men of moderate left views by no means inimical to the United States.

This concrete example reveals the extent to which enlightened opinion in Latin America mistrusts the activities of Private Enterprise Unlimited, and how widely held is the belief that American firms can rely on the backing of the Embassy even when their activities would not appear to be likely to improve the relations between the two countries. This is a field, therefore, in which an objective enquiry might bring about valuable results.

15. — POSITIVE ASPECTS OF AMERICAN ENTERPRISE

An objective report on such negative aspects of American business penetration in Latin American countries would do much to reinforce all that can be said in favour of it. After all, taken all in all, the economic influence of the United States has been a boon to Latin America. It would be a gross lack of sense of proportion as well as of fairness to overlook the fact that Latin America owes to the United States a good deal of material progress and even of intellectual stimulus.

This is so even in countries of predominantly European stock, such as Argentina. It is even more so where labour belongs to the still undeveloped Indian sectors of the population, as for instance in Peru. It cannot be seriously denied that in most cases the standard of salaries and welfare nowadays adopted by American enterprises in Latin America is in general so good that these industrial complexes become true centres of comfort, health and education irradiating their beneficent action beyond their confines. Nor can it be denied that in many cases the private initiative of the American, his know-how and his financial capacity have brought to light zones of wealth which the country itself might have left fallow possibly for another generation.

This positive, fertilizing action of the free enterprise and technical skill of the United States, animated as it is, nowadays, by a more enlightened spirit, deserves to be better known. It probably would be if alongside it other less favourable aspects of the connection did not pretend not to exist by remaining in a discreet penumbra.

16. — MISUSE OF NATIONAL SOVEREIGNTY

The United States should consider it as her primordial interest to study the set of forces at work in the awkward situation that has developed in the world towards her. She could not be more generous than she has proved herself to be from the time of the Marshall Plan to the present day. Millions of dollars and thousands of experts have gone forth to put on its feet again an exhausted world over which her soldiers watch. And yet, the world is sullen. This applies less to Latin America. She is not particularly defended, in a direct way, protected though she is indirectly; nor is much aid forthcoming save in some specific cases such as Bolivia. And yet (I say and *yet*), Latin America is also sullen. Why?

The answer might be best couched in terms of national sovereignty. In a way, sovereignty is to a nation what liberty is to the individual. It might be defined as the right and the power freely to take one's own decisions in all that concerns matters vital to one's own destiny (including the right and the power to define such matters). Now in the discussions, frequent in our day, on the advantage and the possibility of surrendering a certain degree of national sovereignty, one aspect of the question, possibly the most important, is often overlooked. It is best expressed in Vinet's neat dictum: "In order to give oneself one must belong to oneself." How can a nation surrender a sovereignty it does not possess?

Nor does the matter end here. For a nation's sovereignty may be defective in two ways: because the nation is too weak to resist foreign (private or public) pressure, as is the case of most small countries; or because the nation has not enough "being" to resist inner pressures coming from groups smaller but stronger than the nation itself; and this is the case of no less a nation than the United States. In one word, the United States wields more sovereignty over a number of Latin American nations than over some of her own capitalist enterprises. These enterprises are strong enough to usurp the national sovereignty of the United States and so to force her to take decisions to serve their own private or restricted interests, alleging that they are the interests of the United States; and thus armed with the formidable sovereignty of the United States, they overwhelm the weak sovereignty of the Latin American State in question. The material interests of a number of American citizens prosper, and the moral authority of the United States declines.*

I 7. — DICTATORS PREFERRED

There is a Spanish (and French) phrase about frying pans being held by the handle. A handle is, of course, a most convenient feature of frying pans, and one which cooks very much appreciate. The service rendered by a pan-handle to a cook who wants to hold a pan is precisely that which a dictator renders to a firm or foreign power that wants to hold a country. A nation without a dictator is like a pan without a handle. If a number of the aspects of inter-American relations described above are borne in mind, it will now become clear why Private Enterprise Unlimited and the Pentagon are so fond of dictators.

To begin with, they are expeditive. No nonsense about precedents, legislation to be passed through Parliament, sensitiveness to or of public opinion, vested interests that might be injured or any other of the arsenal of arguments and obstacles

---

*See on this subject *Social Change in Latin America Today* by various hands. There are excellent pages on this and other aspects of Inter-American relations in this work; particularly in Professor Adams's essay on Guatemala, pp. 270-1, and 279-280.

an enterprising businessman or a spirited admiral is apt to find in his way when impatiently seeking a contract or a base.

Then, they are relatively cheap. If there is any bribing to do, dealing with one dictator is cheaper, quicker and safer than having to disperse one's effort on a host of politicians and others. As a matter of fact, however, some of these dictators are honest in matters of money. The Lord through some of His creatures (possibly American) has amply granted their prayer, borrowed from the gipsy: "O Lord, I don't ask for money. I only ask to be put where there is plenty." And so they can easily stand on their dignity whenever money is mentioned by name. These honest dictators are often those whose hold on the country is most precarious. For them, the complicity of an American firm, strong at Washington, is more precious by far than mere dollars. If the actual bidder is the Pentagon, of course, so much the better. The dictator will be able to turn to his people and boast of his achievements in foreign policy; the opposition will be disheartened, and the United States will have contributed to screw on tighter the lid of oppression on one concrete people in order the better to fight for freedom in the abstract.

18.—THE CASE OF FRANCO

The case of Franco must be considered first, not only because it is the clearest of all, but because Franco is the model, the encouragement, the base for nearly every Latin American dictator of our day, and finally because the alliance with the Spanish dictatorship has contributed perhaps more than any other error of the United States to shatter the moral authority which only fifteen years ago exalted this great nation as no other had been before.

Spain, like her sister nations in the New World, evinces a tendency to political extremism which roughly favours anarcho-syndicalism on the left and reactionary clericalism-militarism (the "Right") on the right. Socialism in Spain is a *relatively* conservative force, but can become extremist in moments of crisis (as during the autumn and winter of 1935-6) or when outbid by communism. Normally, communism and the Right are fiercely anti-West; and the rest of Spanish opinion, i.e., socialists, anarcho-syndicalists and liberals, are pro-West. This was confirmed during the Second World War, when the pro-West sector suffered indignities, persecution, prison, beatings and even loss of life merely for their loyalty to the West;* while the dictator, chief and agent of the Right, swore to send two million men to defend Berlin for Hitler, sent the Blue Division to Hitler, and congratulated Japan on her victories in Pearl Harbour and Manila.

When the United States signed a treaty of alliance with Franco, the pro-West sector of Spanish opinion felt betrayed. They had undergone years of humiliation and danger out of fidelity to their political beliefs and their loyalty to the West only to find that the West now shook the hand of, nay, embraced their executioner. But that was not all. The humiliation of which they now were the victims at the hands of those they had mistaken for their friends was far deeper than those they had suffered from the Dictator. And this is a point that must be made quite clear.

Since the end of the Napoleonic wars and the loss of her Empire, Spain had chosen a policy of neutrality and isolation from all affairs north of the Pyrenees. Whether she ought to alter course in present-day circumstances or not is arguable; but for a nation to take such a historical step, a free discussion would have been necessary at the forum of public opinion, and a free and conscious decision should have been taken by her representative institutions.

Furthermore, when Admiral Sherman arrived in Spain in the early nineteen-fifties to start negotiations for naval and air bases, it soon became obvious that the Pentagon wanted to acquire and develop a formidable array of Gibraltars in the country, to such an extent that his plan almost amounted to turning the whole of the country into at least a potential Gibraltar. Here

---

*For revealing details of this persecution of the friends of the U.S.A. and Great Britain by Franco, see *Report on Spain* by Emmett Hughes, New York.

again I am not saying that within the world perspective of the day it would have been wrong to accede to the requirements of the Pentagon; all I say is that for such a formidable decision to be taken, a free discussion and an authentic decision by the country *should have been expected and even required by the U.S.A.*

The fact is that the government and people of the United States chose to accept this twofold sacrifice of traditional policy and of sovereignty—from the hands of a despot who consulted no one and decided on his own. That Franco should behave in such an irresponsible fashion was but natural. That the United States should have accepted from him—and from him alone— what only Spain could give is one of the sombre thoughts that blacken the horizon of every liberal Spaniard.

Expedient, convenient, it certainly was. Think of that long pipeline running from Cádiz to Zaragoza for hundreds of miles across private lands and private lands. How long would it have taken under a free régime merely to disentangle the claims for compensation of so many landowners? But here is where the pan-handle comes in. Franco just cut through the title deeds and let the owners complain—after the event. For swift success in bases, give me a dictator.

And the U.S.A. took the dictator with a vengeance. An ambassador was sent who, not content with the merely correct attitude which should have been his as the representative of a free nation in a nation jailed by its army, went out of his way to sing the praises of the jailer in and out of season; and when the U.S.A. invited the Dictator's War Secretary (who happened to be the ex-Commander of the Blue Division and had been decorated by Hitler with the Iron Cross) to visit the U.S.A. President Eisenhower decorated this stout defender of (whose?) liberty with the Order of Merit.

"Ah, but think of it! Franco saved Spain from communism!" This claim is not merely untrue. It is the very reverse of the truth. It can be stated categorically:

1. When the Army rebelled under Franco there was no communist danger in Spain.

2. There was no question of such a danger in the manifestoes and speeches of the rebels.

3. Communist activity (both Spanish and foreign) in Spain during the civil war, highly stimulated by the war itself, was so outrageous that, by the end of the armed conflict, communism in Spain was as good as dead.

4. The Franco régime has brought it back to life, and every year that the régime lasts brings a fresh crop of recruits and a new tide of enthusiasm to the Communist Party.

This flows from a number of reasons:

1. No political activity is allowed; therefore, the only party that can thrive is that which is used to clandestinity and is not worried about funds.

2. Every enemy of the régime is dubbed a communist, which daily increases the popularity of the Communist Party.

3. No outlet is left for the political activities of the centre parties, so that youth seeks the only possibility there is—communism.

4. There is an inherent alliance between communism and the régime in that both consider the liberal centre as their common adversary.

5. There is no free Spain radio talking to Spain in liberal, moderate terms, but the Spanish people can listen to a weekly average of twenty broadcasts in Spanish, Catalan and Basque, from Prague and beyond.

6. To go over to communism releases the anti-American passion generated by what the Spanish people see as "the American betrayal", the going over to Franco after the world war.

"The most the United States can expect of the Spanish people"—a young Spanish scholar in exile said to me in January 1961—"is the attitude of Nasser."

It is doubtful whether to this day the American people realize the devastating harm which such behaviour on the part of the United States does to the moral authority of the Untied States, and therefore to world peace. The jeering smiles with which any favourable comment on the United States is met in the whole of Latin America, where do they come from if not from this despairing cynicism and disbelief? What avails it that the Pentagon has won a few bases in Spain if the United States has lost a continent?

19. — THE CASE OF TRUJILLO*

The Dominican dictator is the senior despot in the world. He has ruled the Dominican Republic for thirty-one years. He was begotten out of Dominican Police by United States Marine Corps as an heir to the absolute power wielded by the Marines during the First World War and the period that ensued. He was not long in securing the heritage, though by no means the methods of the Marines, for he annihilated opposition by the most direct and ruthless tyranny. In the Dominican Republic no one is ever sure of any one, and informers are omnipotent, so, mum is the word, and even that may point to the cemetery if the tune and tone are not found correct.

According to reliable information, Trujillo and his family own 35% of the cultivable land. His fortune is estimated at anything between 500 and 800 million dollars; and there is hardly a job, high or low, private or public, a business or any other activity in his Republic he does not dispose of with the only freedom there is in the nation, which is his.

There can be no doubt whatsoever that Trujillo is the most cruel and unscrupulous tyrant in the Hispanic world; nor that his relations with the United States have been most cordial throughout his tyrannical reign. Trujillo's opponents had been the victims of vendettas in Havana, in Mexico, but also, in at least two cases, in New York, before the world was shocked by the most outrageous case of all, the disappearance of Professor Galindez. A Spanish citizen, a member of the staff of Columbia University, Jesús de Galindez vanished from New York in March 1956 on the eve of presenting a thesis on Trujillo's régime for his D.Phil. degree. His death caused a chain of other deaths, including that of Gerald Murphy, the American pilot who flew Galindez drugged to the Dominican Republic. The United

*Drafted before Trujillo's assassination.

States Department of State has not accepted the account given by Trujillo's government of the death of Gerald Murphy, but the F.B.I. has not yet found out who kidnapped Galindez in 1956. Other departments of the American government have been luckier. The Navy got a base on Trujillo's island; Trujillo's army has been provided with formidable weapons by the United States; two American senators, Eastland (Mississippi) and Jenner (Indiana), spoke before Trujillo's "parliament", praised him and criticized his critics.

It is true that the Navy had to pay for it. In the summer of 1959, when rumours of an imminent landing of a liberation expedition were rife in Ciudad-Trujillo,* the U.S. Navy sent three admirals to the Dominican capital to support the dictator. In 1960, the capital was chosen to give shore leave to 4,000 Marines during manoeuvres in the Caribbean.

On 24th June, 1960, an attempt was made in Caracas on the life of President Rómulo Betancourt. A bomb set off by remote control exploded near his car and killed his chief A.D.C., a guard and a traffic officer. The President escaped with burns. The Venezuelan government lodged a complaint with the Organization of American States accusing the Dominican Republic of aggression against Venezuela by her complicity in the attempt. The Dominican Vice-President, Joaquin Balaguer, issued a strong denial. The OAS, however, at their meeting of Foreign Ministers in San José (Costa Rica) confirmed that the persons implicated in this plot had received "moral support and material assistance from high officials of the government of the Dominican Republic."

The Secretary of State concurred. Indeed he may well have led the van. A discussion of this meeting must be left for a later stage. But there can be no doubt that this scathing condemnation of one of the Pentagon's oldest allies could hardly be favourable to the moral authority of the United States.

---

*The dictator had his name given to the oldest European city in the New World, founded by Columbus' brother with the name of the patron saint of their father, Domenico, in its Spanish form, Santo Domingo.

20.—HAITI

This nation, a Negro republic occupying the western third of the island Columbus named La Española, is an oddity. It is French-speaking and almost wholly African, and its European traditions, despite the French education of its *élite,* is but shallow. It is the outcome of a gradual encroachment on Spanish territory by French and English buccaneers with no European responsible government behind them. True, it became officially French, i.e., a dependency of the French nation and State, at the Treaty of Ryswick (1697), and fairly prosperous for a time, but the introduction of French revolutionary principles in 1789 led to a fierce civil war, which ended in a complete victory for the blacks. These events are at the root of the two prominent features of the country: pride of the black population and the disappearance of the white, who were massacred by the second of the two black leaders, Jean Jacques Dessalines (1804).

From 1915 to 1934, Haiti was occupied by the United States and governed by U.S. Marines. They were benevolent dictators and improved everything except (typically enough of those days) education. When they left, another line of dictators took over, until in 1946, a schoolteacher, Dumensais Estimé, took office most democratically and governed in an enlightened spirit. He was deposed by a general, Magloire, who at the end of his mandate, when planning to have it renewed by force, was ousted by his fellow generals and, after a brief period of vicissitudes, replaced by the present dictator François Duvalier. He is a friend of Trujillo, and no more need be said about him. He also enjoys the friendship of Washington, and has even obtained a mission of U.S. Marines to reconstitute an army which his own ruthless way with his enemies had all but destroyed.

21.—GUATEMALA

For about thirteen years Guatemala was ruled by a dictator, General Jorge Ubico, the willing tool of foreign (mostly American) interests, owners of the banana and coffee estates. Ubico kept the field for the quiet enjoyment of their estates by these foreign companies, prepared nothing and foresaw nothing, in the "after me the deluge" spirit which is characteristic of these selfish dictators. The dictator's American friends and, in fact, dominant partners were as blind as he was to the dangers which such a policy implied.

So blind indeed that they did not even realize the incoherence implicit in their transferring to a country ruthlessly gagged by a dictator the verbal paraphernalia of their war propaganda, including the Four Freedoms and all that. Let us pause for a story. After the Filipinos, with American help, had got rid of Spanish rule, in 1898, there followed a period of American rule. During this period, American schoolmasters expounded and extolled to wide-eyed Filipino boys the wonders of the American way of life, while their fathers frowned at the new rulers who had come as liberators and stayed on as masters. An American school-mistress set her class an essay on the cow; and one of the Filipino boys wrote this immortal piece, a witness to his commendable speed in absorbing American political philosophy: "The cow is an animal on four legs, one in each corner. The cow gives milk. As for me, give me liberty or give me death."

A thousand pities that this story was not known to the men in charge of the Guatemala desk in Washington during the Ubico dictatorship (if such a desk existed in those days), for much trouble, criticism and even bloodshed might have been saved. The Guatemalans heard the Americans say that liberty was good, which was exactly what they thought, and saw them on the best of terms with the dictator Ubico who thought that liberty was bad. The dictator tightened up his hold on the press, but this time there were riots, and on 22nd June, 1944, he fled to New Orleans, where he died soon after, leaving in charge a junta composed of various generals. On 4th July, 1944, the Guatemala Congress selected General Federico Ponce as provisional President. On 22nd October widespread riots, which caused one thousand casualties in the capital, led to his overthrow, and a junta of officers and civilians took charge. On 21st December, 1944, the junta held presidential elections, and a large popular majority elected Dr Juan José Arévalo, a "doctor" who had been living in exile (in Argentina).

Dr Arévalo returned from exile to occupy the seat of power adorned with an aura of liberalism far too big for his actual deserts. During his exile he had kept in close touch with both Peronists and communists; a combination he could easily reconcile because his chief passion seems to have been a fierce anti-Americanism. He began his presidential work by a series of political, social and economic reforms which seemed fair enough in a country where 2% of the population owns 70% of the cultivated land.* But it was soon noticed that the new President remained passive, indeed many thought favourable, when the Communist Party (barely a few thousands) gained control of the leadership of the Trades Unions. Both the CGT (*Confederación General de Trabajadores*) and the CNC (*Confederación Nacional de Campesinos*) passed thus under communist control, by means of a mixture of corruption and terror which a truly objective and liberal executive should and could have easily defeated.

On 28th April, 1947, two and a half years after his inauguration, President Arévalo betrayed his trust by imposing on the country a strict censorship of every form of printed or broad-

---

*Here again, none of the usual "feudal" and "colonial" nonsense. Here is a witness: "One must wonder at the admirable distribution of the land which was instituted under the Spanish rule in many regions of the old Kingdom of Guatemala, thanks to the righteousness and tenacity of missionaries and bishops. In these regions everything was done to ensure that the natives were the owners of the plough-land house, domestic and load animals. Many small pueblos were moreover endowed with communal lands, and in some, even, a kind of reserve bank was created to provide succour for the native landtiller when floods, locusts, fire or other cause ruined their harvests. The land never had better or more numerous owners than in the sixteenth century of our history." The author goes on to describe how in the seventeenth and eighteenth centuries this good order deteriorated, but recalls that nevertheless, at the time of independence, "there remained at least untouchable the communal lands in the small pueblos and an innumerable legion of small landowners."—The Right Rev. Mariano Rossell y Arellano, Archbishop of Guatemala, in *Estudios sobre el Comunismo*, No. 15, January-March 1957, p. 83.

cast opinion, a measure which drove a coach and four through the Constitution he himself had initiated and sworn to uphold. Silence in public life is seldom a forerunner of good deeds. In the summer of 1949, Colonel Francisco Javier Arana was murdered. Who was he? The man whom the Army considered as the true leader of liberalism, as keen an adversary of dictatorship as of communism. The liberal-minded units of the Army rose in rebellion (18th-19th July, 1949) but troops faithful to the President held good and after a struggle which cost forty lives, Arévalo was victorious.

He had, however, to mute his anti-Americanism for a time. During the first half of October 1949, the country was struck by disastrous floods which resulted in the loss of 400 lives, 70,000 left homeless, and an estimated 50 million dollars worth of damage to property. The United States responded with her proverbial generosity. But by then, the Guatemalan Legation in Paris had become the chief liaison centre between the cominform and the Central American communist parties, and the Minister, Victor Manuel Pellecer, was soon promoted a member of Parliament, Secretary for Agrarian affairs and organizer of the armed communist militia.*

When Arévalo died (1950) and a presidential election was called a number of political parties had emerged including the *Partido de Acción Revolucionaria* and the *Partido de Regeneración Nacional*, both favourable to Arévalo's way of doing things; the *Union Democratica*, a moderate party; and the *People's Party*, a studiously vague formation; as well as the *Conservatives*, who of course stood for vested interests with or without a dictatorship. The new President, Jacobo Arbenz Guzmán (10-12th November, 1950), was to prove another Arévalo but more so. He was a 37-year-old Lieutenant Colonel, the son of a Swiss immigrant, and, as events were to show, belonging to the pro-communist wing of the Army. It is important to remember that the Army was divided in its allegiance; that Colonel Arana had been murdered (by whom?) because while he was an anti-communist with a big following in

*Article by Julian Gorkin in *Cuadernos*. Nov.-Dec. 190, No. 54.

the Army he had also been a militant adversary of Ubico's dictatorship; and that the junta which had displaced the dictator had stepped aside to allow the "doctors" to take charge and bring in a parliamentary system. All this should be remembered if one is to understand why and how Arbenz was eventually ousted.

Arbenz had been elected on the strength of a coalition, the National Democratic Front, the motive power of which came from the Communist Party. Whether willing or unwilling, Arbenz became the tool of the communists, who unleashed on the unfortunate country a ruthless terror, the sole means by which so small a party (hardly 3,000) could hope to hold a nation predominantly Catholic.

It is nevertheless important to discriminate between Arévalo's anti-American passion and Arbenz's weakness towards the communists on the one hand, and on the other the political, economic and agrarian reforms which both presidents launched; just as it is necessary to discriminate between the generous policy of the United States towards Guatemala and the way local American business and diplomacy contributed to discredit the U.S.A.

To begin with the latter issue, Guatemala received so much American aid for education, agricultural extension and public health that between 1946 and 1950 the aid from the Office of Agricultural Relations alone amounted to more dollar assistance than to any other Latin American country.*

Nevertheless, the changes brought about by the Arévalo-Arbenz episode are reported in significant terms by one of the best American guides on Guatemalan affairs:

> Since 1954 the newspapers no longer have occasion to report that the American Ambassador has insulted the President of Guatemala. U.S. officials no longer reject even the principle of agrarian reform as dangerous to private property and American interests. Nor do U.S. technical-aid missions

*Arthur T. Mosher, *Technical Cooperation in Latin American Agriculture* (University of Chicago Press) table 2, page 20; quoted by Prof. Adams, *loc. cit.*

push through their programs in the face of contrary arguments advanced by Guatemalan officials. In the pre-Arbenz period, all these things were happening. Many North Americans would explain this change of approach by pointing out that the Guatemalan government is no longer communistic. This, however, is at best a dubious answer and certainly not the whole answer.*

As for the positive work done by the two anti-American Presidents, it cannot be gainsaid. Faults due to prejudice and, under Arbenz, to communist influence were no doubt committed. Arbenz's agrarian reforms were too collectivist for the individualistic peasants. There was no doubt too much Party (with a capital P) politics in the redistribution of land. But the people became aware of the land problem in a way they had never been before, and the post-Arbenz régimes had to take note.

Terror, too much land collectivism, too much interference by the Communist Party, in the end destroyed the popularity, undoubtedly great at first, of the Arbenz régime. It was then, when thus weakened by his errors in home policy and by his subservience to communism, that Arbenz attempted his too ambitious nationalizations: that of the land of the United Fruit Company and that of the International Railway of Central America. On 25th February, 1953, the United Fruit Company was informed that under the Agrarian Reform Law, 234,000 acres of its 300,000 on the Pacific Coast would be expropriated. All appeals having been rejected by the Court, the distribution of the land to about 23,000 peasants began on 15th November, 1953. Official complaints from Washington to the effect that compensation at $600,000 "bears not the slightest resemblances to just evaluation" were rejected as unfounded. And the 172,000 acres owned by the UFC on the Caribbean Coast were also expropriated on 24th February, 1954. The International Railway connecting the two coasts as well as the two frontiers of Guatemala (with Mexico and with El Salvador) was nationalized on 8th October, 1954.

*Prof. Adams, *loc. cit.*

The outcome of this policy was not long to emerge. By 7th April, 1954, the Guatemalan government was already complaining of hostile conspiracies on the part of two former American ambassadors and Trujillo; on 29th June, 1954, it accused President Anastasio Somoza of Nicaragua of allowing the training of armed forces in his own private estate towards an invasion of Guatemala: the leaders being Castillo Armas and General Ydigoras Fuentes, and the weapons being supplied by the United Fruit Company; while a Colonel Carl Studer had been "retired" from the U.S. Army in order to enable him to put himself at the disposal of the UFC. Denials followed from all States concerned.

At the Caracas OAS Conference (1st-26th March, 1954) Secretary of State Dulles's endeavours to secure a condemnation of the communist infiltration into Guatemala were not rewarded for reasons to be discussed later. The Guatemalan Foreign Secretary described Mr Dulles's attitude as a manoeuvre against his country and denounced to "this Conference and to the conscience of America the threats of political aggression and intervention of which Guatemala is a victim".

Things moved rapidly during the following months. On 17th May, 1954, the State Department denounced an important landing in Puerto Barrios (Guatemala) of a cargo of arms coming from Poland. Both President Eisenhower and Secretary Dulles underscored the gravity of the situation; the pro-communist attitude of the Guatemalan government at Caracas and the fact that the military establishment of Guatemala was three to four times the size of that of her neighbours. On 24th May the U.S. government announced that army supplies were being flown to Honduras and Nicaragua. This last State had broken relations with Guatemala on 19th May on the ground of the "communist tendencies of the Guatemalan government". On 17th May, the State Department requested a number of European countries to co-operate in an embargo of arms for Guatemala and to allow a search of their ships on the high seas. Most of them agreed about the embargo but rejected the request for power to search.

By then, the Guatemalan government had announced (2nd June) that "a wide internal conspiracy directed from outside" was afoot, planned by "military technicians separated from the army of another country". On 18th May, the invasion, from Honduras, had begun with Guatemalan forces led by Colonel Castillo Armas. Arbenz appealed to the U.N. Security Council. He complained that leaflets and later arms of Soviet and American make had been parachuted, the former on the city, the latter close to the headquarters of a subsidiary of the UFC. On 19th May, aircraft of American make coming from Honduras and Nicaragua had bombed the capital.

After heated debates and pious resolutions the Security Council decided to step aside in favour of the OAS (25th June, 1954), whose Peace Committee (U.S.A., Argentina, Brazil, Cuba, Mexico) unanimously approved (28 June) a Nicaraguan proposal to send a fact-finding commission to Guatemala. When this commission arrived in Guatemala (30 June), Arbenz had resigned and a cease-fire agreement was being signed with the insurgents. These negotiations took place in El Salvador and finally led to the setting up of a junta headed by Castillo Armas. Its aims would be the eradication of communism and the restoration of democratic government (8th July). Castillo Armas defined his programme as "social justice, education, employment, improved economy and respect for human personality"; "land to the peasant as his own property"; expropriation of big estates, but "the owners will be paid a just price".

Severe anti-communist and anti-Arbenzist measures were adopted at once, including the freezing of the assets of all the leaders of the Arbenz régime. On 25th August, 1954, communism was outlawed in all its forms, and a five-man *National Committee of Defence against Communism* was set up, endowed with formidable powers. A revolt by the Cadets of the Guatemalan Military Academy (2nd August, 1954) which caused 25 deaths and wounded 100 in 24 hours seems to have been due to a feeling of offended pride at the continued separate existence of the "Liberation Army" which had come from Honduras to oust Arbenz. This contingent was dissolved and absorbed into the regular Army. This feeling does not necessarily mean that the Army was hostile to the new régime; rather the reverse; that the Army disliked the idea that a somewhat amateurish and perhaps mercenary body of invaders could have conquered the country in less than ten days if the regular Army had not been ready for a change. A resolution sponsored by Senator Lyndon B. Johnson had been passed by the American Senate on 25th June, 1954, declaring that any interference of communism in the Latin hemisphere had to be prevented.

Castillo Armas had himself "elected" President by open ballot, and a Constitutional Assembly elected (10th October). The opposition did not vote. The new régime was moderate right (perhaps more right than moderate) and the UFC recovered its lands. Arbenz sought refuge in Prague, which puts a final touch to his profuse protestations of independence of communism. In 1957, Castillo Armas was murdered by an officer of his own guard. His successor was General Ydagoras Fuentes. An indication of the new President's political "climate" may well be that in August 1959 his Ambassador in Spain signed an agreement with the Spanish Fascist Foreign Secretary stipulating that a mission of the Spanish Civil Guard would go to Guatemala for three years to organize the Guatemalan Civil Guard.

This long story was worth telling for it shows:

1. That the government of the United States powerfully contributed to overthrow a pro-communist régime in Guatemala;

2. That it did not care to have the fact openly known;

3. That it did not hesitate to rely for this operation on Anastasio Somoza, one of the harshest dictators in Latin America;

4. That in so doing it exposed itself to the charge of opposing communism not because it is the enemy of human liberty but because it is a movement that threatens American (private) interests.

5. That an appeal to the gravity of the world situation in order to counter the charge under No. 4 is bound to lose most of its force for a people deprived of its own liberty, since the threat of communism to liberty is hypothetical, and their lack of liberty is real.

22. — CUBA

Sometime in 1890, a Havana newspaper, *La Fraternidad*, published an article by its owner and editor, Juan Gualberto Gómez, a Cuban mulatto. Its title was "Separatist, Yes. Revolutionary, No". Its theme was that Cuba should cut loose her ties with Spain, but amicably and without recourse to violence. Cuba was then politically a part of Spain, and she elected her own representatives to both houses of Parliament in Madrid. Gómez was prosecuted and jailed—a curious sort of imprisonment, though, during which he writes regularly for the press from his cell. On 12th March, 1891, he appears before the Court (an ordinary civilian Court) on a charge of incitement to rebellion, and the next day he is sentenced to two years, ten months and eleven days in prison. While serving his sentence he goes on writing his articles in his own paper from his cell. He appeals to the Supreme Court, which sits in Madrid, and meanwhile is granted temporary freedom on bail. On 21st November, 1891, the Supreme Court of Spain declares that Gómez, as a Spanish subject, is not guilty since the Spanish Constitution guarantees free expression to all ideas. He was set free. This happened in 1891.

Not a bad prologue for a survey of the experience of independent Cuba. For it suggests the atmosphere that prevailed in those Spanish days. Under Spain, Cuba was casually governed, badly governed, absent-mindedly governed, corruptly governed, but not harshly governed. The sinister reputation of the concentration camps organized by General Weyler during the middle phase of the 1895-98 war should not obscure this fact. These camps were bad enough, though by Nazi or Soviet standards they were pleasure resorts; but the chief point is that they were war measures. In peace time the island was prosperous. Gold currency—unknown at the time in Spain—circulated freely and in abundance. The land was not yet as unevenly distributed as it became later. There were so many small farms that in 1899 (first year of Cuban independence) those of 143 acres or less made up 50% of the total available land; and while a movement towards a greater concentration of sugar estates had set in during the last fifteen years of the Spanish régime, there was as yet no sign of the excessive difference in the standard of living between rich and poor that was to develop later.

With "independence", Cuba passed in fact from Spanish to American dependence; and (as this change came about exactly at the turn of the century) from the relatively slow nineteenth-century rhythm to the swift pace of the twentieth. Men, money, ideas flowed into the island; sugar production rose as the number of estates fell and their individual sizes increased. In 1926-27 about one third of the crop was produced by only twenty of the biggest "centrals". Similar conditions had developed with regard to tobacco and coffee, the two chief industrial crops after sugar. By 1946 the latifundia covered ten times more land than that of the farmers owning 25 acres or less. The big sugar companies and the cattle estates owned between them seventeen million acres. Out of the ten largest sugar landowning companies, the 1st, 3rd, 5th, 6th, 7th, 8th and 10th were American. This should be borne in mind when the question of the special price paid by U.S.A. for "Cuban" sugar is discussed.*

While the general level of prosperity rose, the contrast between rich and poor increased. Huge fortunes were made, but the income of the poorer families did not rise above 200 dollars yearly and 25% unemployment was endemic. The climate, with its rare abundance of sun and water, and a rich earth, makes poverty easier to bear in Cuba than elsewhere; and the island felt happy and carefree to such an extent that it became hard to discipline go-getters, money-makers and adepts of the "tasty life" (*vida sabrosa*). The country, of late, had become a huge tourist resort mostly for leisure and pleasure loving Americans.

It was governed—in a way—by Batista (Fulgencio Batista Zaldívar). A general, of course. But no ordinary one. Usually

*I borrow these data as well as a fair number of subsequent details from "Cuba: A Dissenting Report" by Samuel Shapiro in *The New Republic,* 12th September, 1960, a study which, though at times perhaps too generous and optimistic in favour of Castro, should be read as a conscientious and well informed corrective to much that is being written on the subject.

generals are made out of colonels; this one had been made out of a sergeant; and by no war-minister, but by himself. Why—thought he—must a military junta which ousts a President always be composed of generals? Why not try sergeants? He tried and won.

This happened in 1933. Batista, having ousted the President, donned a colonel's uniform and hoisted to the presidential chair a professor of medicine, Dr Ramón Grau San Martín. The new President did not find favour with the U.S.A.; and so Batista ousted him, and after a period during which he ruled the country from the wings, being possibly too shy because of his too recent sergeanthood, he took the presidency himself, held elections and was elected President under a liberal constitution (1940). At the end of his mandate, his rival Grau San Martín was elected (1944). In 1948, Grau was succeeded by Carlos Prío Socarrás.

By 1952, however, Batista seems to have exhausted his reserves of liberal-democratic patience. He stood as a candidate for the presidential election due that year; but when he realized that he would not be elected, he deposed Prío Socarrás by means of a military coup and declared himself President (10th March, 1952). How could this be possible after eight years of free parliamentary rule? The answer is clear and must be recorded: because the political *élite* of the country failed to gain from public opinion the respect and moral authority required owing to their lack of austerity in the husbanding of the rich island's resources.

This point must be stressed, for it is crucial. In discussing Cuba, much—far too much—criticism must unfortunately be levelled against the United States; but it is essential to realize that (North) American intervention can only worsen evils which are already there. *The trouble in Cuba is essentially a Cuban trouble,* and it is both untrue and unfair to accuse the United States for it or even most of it. To make a situation worse is not to create it. The two administrations, of Grau San Martín and of Prío Socarrás, were corrupt to the core. And, what is even more to the point, the chief denouncer of such corruption, the man who stood for honesty in public life, and (it is generally believed) meant it, was Fidel Castro. He was the Havana chief of the "Orthodox" Party, a splinter group separated from the PRC (*Partido Revolucionario Cubano*), the party in power, as a protest against the prevalent corruption. On 26th June, 1953, Castro, in Santiago, led the first of the armed attempts against Batista. Several others followed until Batista had himself elected in 1954 in a rigged election.

By then he was certain of the unpopularity of his régime and his rule became harsher. Most of the prisoners made by the President's troops during Castro's first attempt died having been allowed to bleed after castration. An organized and systematic terror was launched. Victims of torture and death were numbered in their thousands. The sea rejected mutilated bodies on the shores.

The whole nation was resolutely against the tyrant—all but the communists, who watched events and would not be moved by mere tortures and corpses. The dictator, however, felt confident mostly because he relied on the open and resolute backing of the United States. He knew that "American companies controlled 40% of the island's sugar lands, 80% of the mines and cattle ranches, and, in combination with Shell, substantially all the oil business". He saw shining on his table the gold telephone and stand presented to him by the Cuban Telephone Company for having let it increase its tariffs to its heart's content.* He knew that he could count on the American Ambassador as his best propagandist. He was aware of the importance the Pentagon attached to the naval base in Guantánamo; and he saw with satisfaction the head of his General Staff, General Francisco Tabernillas, embraced before the cameras by the American Ambassador. Batista—so he thought—did not need to worry about trouble.

Yet trouble came. Towards the end of 1956 a group of about eighty exiles led by Fidel Castro in seacraft coming from Mexico succeeded in landing in the province of Oriente. Attacked by

---

*This company did not even bother to call itself by a Spanish name, and on its buildings the name was displayed in English.

9

Batista's forces they were wiped out, all but twelve who managed to take refuge in the Sierra Maestra. This small group
gradually gathered strength and numbers. In the following summer a second rebellion began in the province of Las Villas, led
by the *Directorio de Estudiantes Revolucionarios.*

What was the attitude of the U.S.A. to these events? In
November 1957 Major General Laudon, USAF, flew to Havana
to decorate with the Order of Merit the leader of Batista's Air
Force, fresh from a bombing raid on the city of Cienfuegos. In
the same month, General Shepherd, of the U.S. Marine Corps,
publicly toasted Batista as "a great general, a great president".
Arms were sent to Batista until March 1958; but even then,
American military training missions remained; and when Dr
Miró Cardona, who was the rebels' representative in Miami,
wrote to President Eisenhower (26th August, 1958) about it,
the State Department answered (seven weeks later) that the
training of Batista's men would have to continue owing to
"hemispheric defence needs".

By 1958, Batista was faced with a serious revolt in which the
several branches of the Cuban political tree collaborated in
various degrees, the last to join being the communists. The
two chief fronts were able to effect a conjunction when one of
Castro's lieutenants, Ernesto Guevara, advanced towards Las
Villas (October 1958). The province of Pinar del Río rebelled
at the same time. When Santa Clara fell to the rebels (18th
December) Batista's fate was sealed. At dawn on 1st January,
1959, the dictator flew to safety in the Dominican Republic.

There is only one reasonable explanation of this dramatic
success. It is due not to Castro's strength but to Batista's weakness. Castro's forces were counted in hundreds, and at their
highest peak did not surpass 3,000. Batista's army mustered
40,000 men. Castro's victory was the outcome of terror and
counter-terror. Batista's resistance became so barbarous, and its
weight fell so heavily on the young scions of the middle class that
his own civil service and army deserted him.

This explanation in its turn sets the present Cuban revolution
in its right perspective. It was essentially a middle-class affair,

and from the point of view of the origin of its leaders it is still essentially bourgeois. There can be no question of a workers' revolution, in the communist sense of the word, for the workers were either against Batista and against communism, or they were communists and for Batista, since the *Partido Socialista Popular* (communist) had maintained an ambiguous attitude owing to its policy of collaboration with Batista, pursued since 1939. Of a peasant revolution there could be no question either. The revolt was led by the middle class in the name of liberal-democratic principles; and it was in the name of such principles that Fidel Castro led his men and gained the nation's backing.*

Fidel Castro overnight became the hero not only of Cuba but of every liberal-minded man or people in the world, and hopes rose high of a Cuban régime at last free and honest. Honest it was to be, but not free. Whether at the outset he was a genuine liberal democrat or not, the fact is that Castro soon evinced every one of the features of Left-wing totalitarianism; the last to rally to his camp, the Communist Party of Cuba, were the first to profit by his victory. This may have been due to the influence of that triumvirate of able and resolute communists he brought with him (or who brought him with them). His brother Raul took the armed forces; Ernesto Guevara finances; and Captain Nuñez Jiménez the land. All other parties were driven to the wall; all other men reduced to submission, death or exile. It is doubtful, nevertheless, whether this evolution towards an out and out communism would have been successful if the attitude in Washington had been less smiling towards the dictator and less frowning towards the liberator. Things were fluid at first, and it is not certain that Castro was past winning over. No invitation to visit Washington was sent to Fidel Castro, not even when he let out a broad hint that he wanted to come, and when unofficially invited, he was hardly received as what after all he was, the official leader of a friendly country. President

---

*Such is the view of the observer who has written by far the most temperate, accurate and penetrating study of the Cuban revolution known to me: "Castro's Cuba" by Theodore Draper in *Encounter*, No 90, March 1961; and several other equally good studies.

Eisenhower who had decorated a good half dozen dictators with
the Order of Merit was away. Air raids organized by anti-Castro
exiles from Florida were not prevented until they had to be
because an American citizen was involved in one of them.*

The outward events are too well known to need recording.
Castro became more and more virulent against the U.S.A., and
in this way, he all but achieved a U.S.A. "sacred union" against
him, thus throwing away the goodwill he undoubtedly enjoyed at
first in a good half of American public opinion. This may or
may not have been deliberate. It certainly was unfortunate.

Among other reasons, because this anti-American fever
which his long speeches generated imparted an unnecessarily
virulent quality to his agrarian reform, so his expropriation of sugar lands took on the aspect of an aggression. It was—
or should have been—an indispensable and overdue operation
of agrarian revolution, such as nearly the whole continent should
carry out as soon as possible, precisely to save itself from communism. Its impact, though, was that of an act of cold war.
American interests were declared to be gravely injured, a phrase
dangerously vague and even equivocal insofar as "American" in
this case meant "of some Americans" while the sonorous
phrase seemed to imply that the whole American nation had
suffered.

Now, from the point of view of Cuba, these private American
interests meant 40% of her sugar production, but from the point
of view of the U.S. this business of Cuban sugar was a mere
fleabite. Furthermore, the expropriation was made on the basis
of payment in 4.5% bonds redeemable in twenty years. It was
really a purchase, not a confiscation. But there was a catch in
it, i.e., who should value the land. The catch was by no means

---

*It is often claimed that Castro wanted and actually sought
economic aid from the U.S.A. and that it was his failure to obtain it
in Washington that forced him to cross the line. This does not seem
to be well founded. Rather the reverse. In a letter to *The New Leader*
(2nd December, 1961) Theodore Draper proves that Castro did not
ask for money and that indeed he rejected the offers made to him by
Robert B. Anderson on the strength of the statements made by Castro
himself and by three of his economic advisers of the period.

in the fact that the land would be valued by the government; rather the reverse. The catch was in the fact that the government would take at its face value the companies' own valuation of their own land. And as these lands were deliberately under-valued by their owners for taxation purposes, the American companies had their fingers caught.

Nor is this all; for the American sugar companies working in Cuba have derived immense benefits both in capital and in interest from their investments there. The weakness and corruption prevailing in the island for generations had allowed all kinds of land appropriation and "purchase" under all too favourable conditions; particularly during the period of American occupation which followed the end of the Spanish-American war. A case is quoted of 122,000 acres in the Province of Oriente purchased by an American company for one hundred dollars. And it is estimated that owing to the dependence of Cuban sugar economy on American quotas, the companies allowed about three million acres of the most fertile land in the world to lie fallow with an underpaid and unemployed population looking on.

The picture is therefore by no means all black here and all white there. But the fact cannot be gainsaid that Cuba has become a communist outpost in the New World. And it is idle to entertain any illusions as to what this means for the future of Latin America and of the world.

23. — COLLECTIVE ACTION

1. The root of all collective action in the American continent must be found in the necessity felt in Washington for some sort of institution to canalize and so to speak administer the natural hegemony of the United States over Latin America. This would explain why the Pan-American Union which was the first outcome of this tendency did not, in spite of its prefix, include Canada. The first name of the new body was International Union of American Republics, and its purpose "the prompt

collection and distribution of commercial data and information".
An office was to represent it in Washington under the name of
"the commercial bureau of the American republics". These
decisions of the first international conference of American States
held in Washington (29th March, 1890) were developed in a
second conference held in Mexico (29th January, 1902) provid-
ing that the Bureau should be led by a governing board
composed of the diplomatic representatives of the American
republics in Washington under the chairmanship of the Secretary of State. The word "commercial" was dropped from the
title, which became "the international bureau of the American
republics". No significant change took place in Rio de Janeiro
at the third conference (19th August, 1906); but at Buenos
Aires (1910) the Bureau became the Pan-American Union, and
the institution, Union of American Republics. In Santiago de
Chile (1923) the rule that reserved for the Secretary of State
the Chairmanship of the Board was abolished and both chairman and vice-chairman became elective.

This trend towards more equality within the Union was to
reassert itself time and again during the following conferences,
even though it was bound to remain mostly formal. There was
and still is a fundamental difference in power of all kinds between the one strong and the many weak partners that from the
outset was bound to inflict a kind of lameness on the institution,
and to hamstring, inhibit or even misdirect many an initiative
of the United States within the organization.

The Second World War submitted the Union to a severe test.
The Conference of Havana (Summer 1940) adopted a Cuban
resolution putting under collective Pan-American trusteeship
any American possessions of European powers conquered by
Germany while plans for a hemisphere-wide disposal of export
surpluses, prepared by the government of U.S.A., did not go
beyond pious general resolutions. The war nevertheless drew
North and South together whenever nazi or fascist ideologies did
not hinder it. Thus in the Rio Conference (14-21st March,
1942) the pro-Axis tendencies prevailing in Argentina at the
time limited the resolution to a general declaration of solidarity,

though a number of nations openly declared against Nazi Germany. The Conference did however set up a Pan-American Political Defence Committee, including representatives of Argentina, Brazil, Chile, Mexico, Uruguay, U.S.A. and Venezuela, which met in Montevideo (15th June, 1942) and assumed powers to deal with Nazi infiltration and propaganda. An Inter-American Defence Board was also organized in Washington (30th March, 1942).

The Conference held in Mexico (February 1945) took place in the absence of Argentina, then still dissentient from the fold. It adopted the document known as the "Act of Chapultepec", in which it was declared that an act of aggression against any of the American Republics would be considered as an act of aggression against every one of them. Resolutions of a similar tenor were adopted on political and military defence, economic questions and social and cultural relations. The fact that the American Republics attached to this document the value of a charter of regional organization was, at their request, recognized in San Francisco during the drafting of the Charter of the United Nations Organization.

On the whole the Pan-American Union had successfully undergone the test of the world war. Its most severe trial may well have been the pro-Axis tendencies of certain powerful sectors in Argentina, and their logical consequence—Peronism. Perón, however, was an empiricist, ready ultimately to parley and even to toast arm in arm with State Department empiricists such as Undersecretary Holland. It was precisely the peculiarities of the Argentine attitude under Perón which delayed for nearly two years the Pan-American Conference at last held in Petropolis, above Rio de Janeiro, on 18th-25th October, 1947, in which a treaty of mutual defence was concluded in pursuance of the resolutions of Chapultepec. The treaty was successfully concluded (30th August, 1947); but efforts made by some delegations, notably the Cuban, for some kind of Marshall Plan for the New World were rejected by Secretary of State Marshall on the ground that the case of Europe was more urgent. The stress had unfortunately been put on aid; a better study of the case might have counselled other ways for improving the economic ties between North and South.

Such is the evolution which ultimately led to the Organization of American States, launched at Bogotá (29th May, 1948). It is perhaps symbolical of the whole theme that this step was taken at a Conference which had just had to adjourn its debates owing to a violent popular revolt, in actual fact an explosion of anti-Americanism (9th April). Its origin was national enough, the murder of Señor Gaitán, the liberal leader; but the angry crowds favoured the American Embassy with their irate attacks and though Secretary of State Marshall himself pointed to communism as the motive power and inspiration of the rising, the fact is not certain. One of the trouble makers was a young Cuban, Fidel Castro.

During the first phase of the Conference the question of economic co-operation was revived, notably by the Mexican delegation, which suggested the creation of an Inter-American Bank for financing underdeveloped countries and an Inter-American Economic and Social Council. Insofar as these prospects aimed at solving the problem through institutions rather than through mere loans, they deserved a better hearing than they got from Mr Marshall.

After the interval caused by the riot the Conference met again on 14th June, 1948, and adopted a Charter of the Organization of the American States amounting to a codification under UNO of the regional arrangements approved in several preceding conferences on defence, economy and culture.

Apart from minor decisions on unrest in the Caribbean, the next important step was the Declaration of Washington (3rd June, 1951) adopted by the Conference of Foreign Ministers of the OAS on the last day of their meeting in the American capital. It was a document urging strong home action and equally determined inter-American co-operation to defend the continent "against the aggressive activities of international communism". It did not, however, venture beyond generalities in the economic field; but initiated a series of unfortunate references to "ensuring respect for the fundamental freedoms of

man" in documents signed by dictators who daily trampled upon
them.

It was this tension between deeds and words which dogged
the efforts of the American Delegation at the Caracas
(10th-17th July, 1954) Conference of OAS. Costa Rica
refused to attend owing to the then totalitarian character of the
Venezuelan government; and when Mr Dulles tried to mobilize
Latin American feeling against communism in the name of
"our ideals", Arbenz's Foreign Secretary, Guillermo Toriello,
found a ready ear for his claim that Dulles's draft resolution was a
pretext to intervene in his country. Dulles was forced to accept
a wording that removed any fear of unilateral action in a concrete case of threat of communism, and also to add to the
declaration a reiteration of "the faith of the peoples of America
in the effective exercise of representative democracy", which
the representatives of dictatorial governments signed without
turning a hair. And what is more, by nineteen votes to nil,
Guatemala abstaining, the Conference passed a resolution on
human rights which many a man in the prison cells and torture
chambers of Pérez Jiménez must have found nauseating.

Thus, Latin American public opinion went on being buffeted
now on its moral now on its material side, by the short-sighted
attitude of the Big Brother. An Inter-American Conference
convened in Petropolis (22nd November, 1954) did not move
the American Secretary of the Treasury, Mr Humphreys, beyond granting an extension of U.S.A. lending policies, but he
pointed out that the loans were intended to encourage private
enterprise and not to displace it. Two American Congressmen
present, Senator Smathers and Representative Fulton, declared
their dissent from this niggardly policy.

But if deeds were short, words were long. On 21st-22nd
July, 1956, the presidents of the 21 American republics met in
Panama to celebrate the 150th anniversary of the Congress of
Panama convened by Simón Bolívar in the same city. One more
Declaration, after so many, was drafted and signed by the 21.
It begins with a downright historical howler, to wit that
Bolívar's Congress had "constituted the first collective manifes-

tation of Pan-Americanism".* Having delivered themselves of
this sonorous error, the 21 presidents, headed by Mr Eisenhower, proceed no less sonorously to assert that "the destiny of
America is to create a civilization that will give tangible meaning to the concept of human liberty, etc., etc.," and the paper
is signed by no less than eight ruthless dictators.

Thus was gradually dwindling into nothingness the faith of
Latin American enlightened public opinion in solemn words and
their utterers; and by way of consequence, in the United States
and her professions to stand for liberty and the dignity of man.
Then, what the more far-seeing observers apprehended did
happen. During one of those futile good-will tours in South
America (6th-13th September, 1958) Vice-President Nixon
met with a cold reception almost everywhere, and a truly insult-
ing, angry and somewhat formidable explosion of anti-American
passion in Lima and in Caracas. Communism? Who doubts that
the communists were there, that they were the most eager and
violent? But the demonstrations were by no means just communist. They released a feeling, partly unjustified and unfair,
but a real feeling wider and deeper than mere East-West tension
could inspire.

President Eisenhower's first reaction was somewhat military
(four companies of marines and parachutists were sent to
Caribbean bases) but in itself obsolete and short-lived. Vice-
President Nixon's attitude, cool and dignified throughout,
pointed to the right diagnosis. President Kubitschek of Brazil
underscored it in a letter to President Eisenhower; and Mr
Dulles was able to put the final touches to the idea, both during
a visit to Rio (4th-5th August, 1958) and during a meeting of
Foreign Ministers which took place in Washington on 23rd-
24th April, 1958. A study was at once initiated to set up an
inter-American economic development institution. In the end,
not one but two such institutions were set up (April 1959);
the Inter-American Development Bank and the Fund for Special
Operations; the first with a capital of $850 million divided into

---

*Bolívar wanted a "Spanish" affair in its narrowest sense, without
Brazil, Haiti or the U.S.A.

85,000 shares; the U.S.A. taking $150 million of paid-in capital and $200 million of capital payable on call, the rest of both capitals to be subscribed by the remaining republics. The organization of the fund was similar.

This was the first substantial step taken by the U.S.A. on the path of an institutional solution of the material problems of the Southern half-continent. By then, however, the moral situation had seriously deteriorated and, as a consequence of the Cuban revolution, tensions grew between Red Dictator Castro and Black Dictator Trujillo which led to the abortive attempt at invasion of the Dominican Republic (19th June, 1959) and the diplomatic break between the two countries. Trujillo explained to the OAS (17th July) that Venezuela was collaborating in this Cuban conspiracy. Relations between these two countries went from bad to worse until the tension culminated in the attempt on President Betancourt already described.

The rapid evolution of the Cuban revolution towards communism had estranged Castro and Betancourt: Castro had accused the U.S. before the Security Council of UNO (11th July, 1960) of pursuing "a policy of intervention in Cuba's domestic affairs and of economic aggression", and the issue had been referred by the Council to the OAS. As President Betancourt had brought before the OAS the situation in the Dominican Republic, the institution found itself faced with a somewhat even-keeled problem: Trujillo versus Castro.

Such was in fact the agenda of the meeting of OAS Foreign Ministers which took place in Bogotá on 15th-22nd October, 1960. On the one hand, the Venezuelan accusation against the Dominican Republic for alleged complicity in the attempt on President Betancourt's life; on the other, a Cuban-American dispute. The very symmetry of the situation permitted vistas of a kind of *do ut des*: the U.S.A. might suggest, if, of course not say, "I'll give you Trujillo and you give me Castro". This may have been a kind of rough sketch of expected events. But events did not turn out quite as expected. Trujillo was found guilty of "acts of aggression and intervention against Venezuela"; and diplomatic relations were severed by eleven nations, including the U.S.A.; sanctions were decreed and, for once, the U.S.A. Undersecretary of State Herter went further than the other republics: Mr Herter proposed that "a special inter-American committee should be set up to ensure free elections in the Dominican Republic and foster the growth of true democracy in that country". This proposal did not prosper. It is a pleasure to record an hour when the U.S.A. proposed the right, courageous and intelligent way, and the error—not following—was on the others.

This curious state of affairs may have been due to a convergence of three causes. Some delegates were not as enamoured as all that of "true democracy" and "free elections". Other delegates may have shrunk from a precedent which brought in foreign intervention (though as proposed by Mr Herter it was unimpeachable); other States were conscious that they might open the door to intervention in Cuba, a development which, they knew, public opinion in Latin America would not countenance.

For this was the harvest of thistles for the United States. After years and decades of relying on black dictators, the U.S.A. came to the American Forum to condemn at once the first red dictator that had blossomed out in the continent. Despite everything, Castro was immediately popular in the whole of Latin America, not least because he was seen as a kind of David facing and even challenging the giant Goliath. And the San José Conference just voted pious hopes and good offices.

IV

SOVIET AND CHINESE ASPECTS

I. — HISTORICAL SURVEY

W H E N the bolsheviks seized power in Russia and their
eyes scanned the world from the imperial height, what can have
been their attitude towards Spain and the Hispanic continent
beyond? A certain historical link between Russia and the Latin
American empire existed already. It is best recalled from the
pages in which Karl Marx himself recorded it. Here is what the
future apostle of the Soviet Union has to say on this picturesque
episode in the course of an article dated London 15th August,
1854 and published in the *New York Daily Tribune* on 1st
September, bearing on what for Marx were recent events:

> Should anybody doubt that Russia really had a hand in
> Peninsular affairs, let me remind him of the affair of the *Isla
> de Leon*. Considerable bodies of troops were assembled at
> Cadiz, in 1820, destined for the South American colonies.
> All at once the army stationed on the Isle declared for the
> Constitution of 1812, and its example was followed by troops
> elsewhere. Now, we know from Chateaubriand, the French
> Ambassador at the Congress of Verona, that Russia stimu-
> lated Spain to undertake the expedition into South America,
> and forced France to undertake the expedition into Spain. We
> know, on the other hand, from the message of the United
> States President, that Russia promised him to prevent the
> expedition against South America. It requires, then, but little
> judgment to infer as to the authorship of the insurrection of
> the Isla de Leon. But I will give you another instance of the
> tender interest taken by Russia in the commotions of the

Spanish Peninsula. In his *Historia política de la España moderna* (Barcelona, 1849), Señor de Marlinani, in order to prove that Russia had no reason to oppose the constitutional movement of Spain, makes the following statement:

There were seen on the Neva Spanish soldiers swearing to the Constitution [of 1812] and receiving their banners from imperial hands. In his extraordinary expedition against Russia Napoleon formed from the Spanish prisoners in France a special legion who, after the defeat of the French forces, deserted to the Russian camp. Alexander received them with marked condescension, and quartered them at Peterhoff, where the Empress frequently went to visit them. On a given day Alexander ordered them to assemble on the frozen Neva, and made them take the oath for the Spanish Constitution, presenting them at the same time with banners embroidered by the Empress herself. This corps, thenceforth named "Imperial Alexander", embarked at Kronstadt, and was landed at Cadiz. It proved true to the oath taken on the Neva, by rising, in 1821, at Ocaña for the re-establishment of the Constitution.

While Russia is now intriguing in the Peninsula through the hands of England, it, at the same time, denounces England to France. Thus we read in the *New Prussian Gazette* that England has made the Spanish revolution behind the back of France.

What interest has Russia in fomenting commotions in Spain? To create a diversion in the West, to provoke dissensions between France and England, and lastly to seduce France into an intervention. Already we are told by the Anglo-Russian papers that French insurrectionists of June constructed the barricades at Madrid.

In a later article published by the *Tribune* on 2nd December, 1854, Marx returns to the subject:

In our day it has been affirmed by English writers, with an express allusion to the present Spanish revolution, on the one hand that the movement of 1820 was but a military conspiracy, and on the other that it was but a Russian intrigue. Both assertions are equally ridiculous. [...] As to Russian intrigue, it is not to be denied that Russia had her hands in the business of the Spanish revolution; that, of all the European powers, Russia first acknowledged the Constitution of 1812, by the treaty concluded in Weleski Luki, on July 20, 1812; that she first kindled the revolution of 1820, first denounced it to Ferdinand VII, first lighted the torch of counter-revolution on several points of the Peninsula, first solemnly protested against it before Europe, and finally forced France into an armed intervention against it. Monsieur de Tatischeff, the Russian Ambassador, was certainly the most prominent character at the Court of Madrid—the invisible head of the camarilla. He had succeeded in introducing Antonio Ugarte, a wretch of low station, at Court and making him the head of the friars and footmen who, in their back-staircase council, swayed the sceptre in the name of Ferdinand VII. By Tatischeff, Ugarte was made Director-General of the expeditions against South America, and by Ugarte the Duke of San Fernando was appointed Foreign Minister and President of the Cabinet. Ugarte effected from Russia the purchase of rotten ships, destined for the South American Expedition, for which the order of St Ann was bestowed upon him.

These glimpses of European history in the days of imperial Russia suggest an attitude not without parallel in our day, more complex though our international life has become. This Russian tradition, though, may well have vanished with the official class which harboured and nurtured it, even if the instinct and attitude remained, like a grin after the smile had gone. On the other hand, the bolsheviks brought with them a closer contact with the Spanish class-struggle and its protagonists. In 1868, the year of the revolution which dethroned Isabel II, Farinelli and, later, Lafargue (Marx's son-in-law) visited Spain, where a working-class movement had been gathering momentum for years.

These two visits were symbolical of much that was to come: for Farinelli brought with him the seed of Bakunin's anarchism and Lafargue that of Marx's socialism. The two Spanish branches of the movement parted company when Marx and

Bakunin separated their hosts at the Hague (1872). The Socialist or Marxist Movement gave forth the *Partido Democratico Socialista Obrero,* founded in 1884; as well as the *Union General de Trabajadores,* its industrial counterpart, which came to life in 1888. The Bakunists, temperamentally and doctrinally less prone to institutions, dispersed their efforts in strife and violence, particularly in 1873, when their activity is chastised in scathing articles by Engels published in *Der Volkstaat* (30th October, 1872; 5th November, 1873). It is not without relevance to recall that the socialists styled themselves *autoritarios* and the anarchists *anti-autoritarios.*

These two historical trends come together as Lenin scans the world with the eyes of a Red Tsar in 1917. On the one hand the importance of Spain as a key nation and territory on the chessboard of power policy; on the other, the sensibility of the Spanish people to matters of social justice and dreams of social revolution, and their tendency to split into pessimistic, patient, authoritarian socialists and optimistic, impatient, anti-authoritarian anarchists.

Communism made but little headway in Spain. It was abhorrent to the anarchists, who to this date remain its resolute adversaries there as well as in Latin America; and as for the socialists, it is doubtful whether Marxism ever was as essential a philosophy to them as it is to their French or German comrades. The first confederation of labour unions set up in Spain (1854) chose for its name *Union de Clases,* hardly an orthodox Marxist name; and when shortly after Lenin's triumph (1917), the Spanish socialists sent a mission to Moscow to look at the new-born infant phenomenon, Fernando de los Rios, one of the three delegates, a humanist as much as a socialist, had a revealing talk with Bukharin. "Yes," argued the Spaniard, "I see all that, but what happens to liberty?"—"Liberty?"—asked the Bolshevik theoretician unwittingly sharpening the knife that was going to sever him from life—"Don't you understand that we are creating an orthodoxy that admits of no contradiction?" And de los Rios retorted: "Nothing new to us. We tried that under Philip II."

This rather stubborn peculiarity of Spanish socialists may have been one of the causes of the attitude the Soviet Union and Party were to take towards Latin America. Their mediocre knowledge of the land and its character and history is another.* In the circumstances, it was but natural that the Marxist revolutionary bias inherent in communism should have led Moscow to the conclusion that all communist work in Latin America would take on not only a pro-Native but an anti-Spanish turn.

This approach to Latin America was possibly not the best in the case of countries almost wholly European, such as Argentina, Uruguay and Costa Rica, perhaps even Chile; but it offered strong advantages everywhere else. The "Spaniard" is the landowner and the employer; he is either the Catholic or the liberal; he stands for the establishment; while communism would naturally seek its support in the landless or land-hungry peasant, the worker, an anti-religious view of life and a general disintegration of every established order whatsoever.

2. — LATIN AMERICA IN SOVIET PERSPECTIVE

While it would be rash to assert that the Soviet Union at first neglected Latin America, it is doubtful whether that part of the world loomed very large in its eyes even as late as 1925 when Stalin defines communist policy towards colonial and dependent peoples in a speech delivered at the newly created Communist University for Oriental Workers (18th May, 1925). The very word "Oriental" betrays a peculiar perspective looking away from America. Furthermore, the adversary then was still Great Britain, the ruler of India, Burma, Malaya, the Middle East and Egypt; while the United States had not yet climbed to that top where one gets shot at. Nevertheless, the way Stalin there

*The article on Bolívar contributed by Karl Marx to the *New American Cyclopedia* (1858) is a perfunctory performance based only on French and English sources if not altogether unreliable, at any rate far from sufficient.

defines the communist programme easily applies to Latin America:

1. To win over to communism the best elements of the working class and to set up autonomous communist parties;

2. To set up a national revolutionary block of workers, peasants and intelligentsia, pitted against the block of national, conciliatory upper middle class and imperialism;

3. To ensure the supremacy of the proletariat [read of the Communist Party] within this block;

4. To struggle with a view to liberating the rural and urban lower middle class from the influence of the national, conciliatory upper middle class.

5. To ensure the compenetration of the movement of emancipation of these colonial and semi-colonial peoples with the proletarian movements of advanced countries.

There seems to be at the time as yet a certain vagueness about all these "colonial and dependent peoples"; which explains why one often finds India and Latin America bracketed together in Soviet papers and bureaucracies. Thus, after the Spanish Civil War (1936-39) the India-Latin America-Spain Department of the Comintern is entrusted to José Díaz, the Secretary of the Spanish Communist Party. This decision is significant in that it emphasizes the non-European approach to Latin America in Moscow. The fact that the department is entrusted to a Spaniard does not carry much weight in this context. It is well known that even in Spain, even during the Spanish Civil War, Moscow never allowed Spanish communists to assume a leading role. So far as communism was concerned, the Spanish Civil War was led by Togliatti, Gerö and Stepanov, an Italian, a Hungarian Jew, and a Bulgarian(?). As for José Díaz's control of his Comintern department, here is what his own political secretary wrote at the time: "I suspect, I suspect vaguely, that José Díaz, Secretary of the Executive Committee of the Communist International and responsible for India, Latin America and Spain, and I, his political secretary and representative of the

Spanish Communist Party [in the Comintern] are in actual fact the political secretaries of Stepanov and Gerö."*

This survey of events during the first years of the Soviet Union suggests that:

(*a*) Moscow (both State and Party) tended vaguely to place Latin America among the "colonial and dependent" peoples;

(*b*) That it was prone to stress the non-European element in Latin America;

(*c*) That it did not neglect Latin America but granted a higher priority to Asia, and the Middle East; in general to British rather than American "dependencies";

(*d*) That it did not trust Spanish communists and preferred to act in the Spanish-speaking world through any other kind of European, in fact, as we are to see, even Asians.

3. — HOW IT ALL BEGAN AND WHERE†

It all began in Mexico. In a sumptuous residence of one of the best quarters in Mexico City (Colonia de Roma) there suddenly and mysteriously turned up a rich Indian who lived like a prince (1918). He spoke of nationalism, of his own country groaning under British tyranny and so forth. He did now and then venture into socialism; but of communism, not a word. He spoke Spanish fluently.

This princely Indian was no other than Manabendra Nath Roy, the prominent Indian communist; and his mission consisted in organizing communism in Latin America. Notice the choice of an Indian for such a mission, and the country, Mexico, precisely where the Indian and Mestizo might with some justification be considered the most receptive to revolutionary influences.‡

*Enrique Castro Delgado, *J'Ai perdu ma foi a Moscou*, Paris, 1950.

†I owe most of the concrete facts and figures of this narrative to *La Ingerencia Rusa en Mexico (y Sudamerica)* by Rodrigo García Treviño, Mexico, 1959.

‡It may well be, however, that by then Roy was not yet an agent of Moscow. He joined the Third International in the following year.

He seems to have been an active participant in a National Socialist Congress which met in Mexico City on 25th September, 1919, in which he moved a resolution, which was adopted, "to spread the idea of bringing about the defeat of capitalism through the conquest of political power by industrial means in order to attain a transitory stage consisting of the dictatorship of the proletariat".

A Mexican working-class movement had already been active for some time. Its beginnings had been anarchist, under a leader, Ricardo Flores Magón; and as early as 1906 Flores and his friends had founded the Grand Circle of Free Workers. By 1912, the movement has gathered weight and responsibility and founded its home, the *Casa Mundial*; so that when towards 1915 the Mexican people have to choose between the brigand Villa and Venustiano Carranza, the man intent on consolidating and canalizing the revolutionary movement into a constitutional State, the workers affiliated to the *Casa Mundial* back Carranza and form themselves into Red Battalions. In 1938 the CROM (*Confederacion Regional Obrera Mexicana*) is born. It was at this point that the 1917 revolution brought Lenin to power and a year later, Roy to Mexico. But the second time the Indian "prince" came empowered to set up the *Pan-American Agency of the Communist International* in Mexico (1920).

There existed already in the city a "Marxist Red Group" whose members were Francisco Cervantes, Mauro Tabón and Nicolás Cano. When, however, Zinoviev sends Roy to Mexico on his second trip (1920), and the *Partido Comunista Mexicano* is set up, the Executive Committee reveals new men: José Rubio, José C. Valadés, M. Paley and Felipe Leija Paz. The party was so far little more than an embryo. It seems, however, to have been generously provided with funds by the Pan-American Agency of the Communist International.

Thus irrigated by Moscow, communist associations of all kinds blossom out suddenly, with all kinds of names and purposes, of youths, of intellectuals, of workers, of peasants; and to make confusion worse confounded, a swarm of foreign communists invade the land, all claiming a share in the leadership. A

Red Radical Convention meeting in Mexico on 15th February, 1921, gave vent to a number of discussions bred by such an abundance of leaders.

Then Zinoviev sent another missionary: this time a Japanese. The link between Latin America and the non European peoples remained alive in the imagination of the Moscovite chiefs.* Sen Katayama, like Roy, was a recent convert to communism from socialism, for it was not until 1921 that he had become an adept. Katayama was given two acolytes, one, a Russian, Borodin, the other, an American, Robert Habermann. As a liaison officer for relations with political and intellectual circles, Katayama disposed of a young Russian woman: Natacha Mihailovna. His only confidential Latin American collaborator seems to have been Victorio Codovilla, to this day a well-known Argentine communist leader, of Italian origin.

The party was small but active, and, under the benevolent neutrality of a government that did not seem alive to the dangers of communism, it founded two or three "Communist colonies" which failed as such but perhaps less so as propaganda stunts. It also organized a *Union of Communist Painters* under the guise of "Technical and Plastic Workers", a door through which famous Mexican painters, chief of them, Diego Rivera, joined the Party. By 1st January, 1928, the Mexican Communist Party comprised about one thousand members.

President Calles was the first Latin American head of State to recognize the Soviet Union, and the first Soviet Minister sent to Mexico was Alexandra Kollontay† (1926). With the establishment of the Legation, the generously irrigated though tender plant began to blossom out, and the usual bait, a trip to Europe and Russia, all expenses paid, began to dangle before intellectuals and labour leaders. The Soviet Union saw in the Mexican revolution a forerunner of the communist revolution which she

---

*This would of course have delighted Columbus, who dubbed "Indians" the aborigines of America because he thought he was either in India or in Cipango, i.e., Japan (which for him was but an island on the coast of India).

†I met her in Geneva on her return and she was more enthusiastic about Mexico itself than about the communists she found there.

expected sooner or later everywhere. The sixth congress of the Third International instructed the Latin American Communist Parties to step up their revolutionary propaganda. These instructions aimed at the U.S.A. and were in the nature of a threat or counter offensive, for at the time the Soviet Union was impressed by the dangers lurking behind the Kellogg Pact. Needless to say, such dangers were purely imaginary.

4. — THE BEGINNING OF THE CONTINENTAL NETWORK

On 11th December, 1927, a meeting took place in Moscow to celebrate the tenth anniversary of the Bolshevik revolution. It was attended by delegates from Argentina, Brazil, Chile, Colombia, Cuba, Ecuador, Mexico and Uruguay. This meeting denounced the Pan-American Federation of Labour as "an instrument of Wall Street" and called a rally of the "working masses" against "the imperialism of the United States and the aggression of the Latin American bourgeoisie". They pledged themselves to work towards the setting up of "a single international grouping of the unions of all countries, races and continents", and to do all in their power to call a meeting of Unions in Montevideo in 1928. This resolution was almost certainly inspired by Losovsky, one of Moscow's specialists for Latin American affairs.

The meeting adumbrated in the Moscow resolution took place in Montevideo on 10th April, 1928. Losovsky was present. He spoke in a tone of prudence and philosophical detachment about the need to be modest and not to expect that the social revolution was round the corner. This unexpected wisdom was due to the fact that by then the Soviet Union was in urgent need of American machinery which she was buying from her naïve (or shortsighted?) adversary for many millions of dollars.

Thus did the Soviet Union lead by the nose her creatures in Latin America, making them blow now hot now cold on "Yankee imperialism" as suited her purpose. On 18th-26th May, 1929, a Communist Assembly met in Montevideo in order to constitute the *Confederación Sindical Latino-Americana*. Its tone was fiercely "anti-imperialist". It would appear that Comrade Mikoyan had already bought all he wanted from the U.S.A.

On 1st-12th June, 1929, the First Latin American Communist Conference met in Buenos Aires. It was attended by 28 delegates belonging to the Communist Parties of Argentina, Brazil, Bolivia, Colombia, Cuba, Ecuador, El Salvador, Guatemala, Mexico, Panama, Paraguay, Peru, Uruguay and Venezuela. Victorio Codovilla represented the Latin American secretariat of the Comintern. He was, however, closely watched by Comrade Luis, who was no other than Stepanov, one of the political secretaries of Manuilsky, the true power behind Dimitrov in the Comintern. Under Stepanov's leadership, the Conference classed the Mexican revolution as a merely democratic middle-class affair, and stressed the need for a more thoroughgoing social revolution based on the alliance of workers and peasants and the conquest of power through infiltration into political parties and labour unions.

5. — COMMUNISM AT THE OUTBREAK OF THE SECOND WORLD WAR

Mexico

The working-class organization had evolved considerably since the arrival of Roy and Katayama in the 'twenties. The CROM had disintegrated. It is doubtful whether it ever was a genuine association of workers conscious of their class and interests. Its leader, Luis N. Morones, was a flamboyant and picturesque Spaniard (from Asturias) who lived like a Roman Emperor, one must assume, on his wards' fees. I well remember the evening he organized in my honour(?) in his country estate where he enjoyed life in a luxurious mansion within a luxuriant park, ample enough for his garage, stables, several pavilions and a theatre. A review was shown on the stage, and I was assured that the evening would have been far more exciting and spectacular had Morones been less inhibited by his visitor, a Spanish Oxford professor as he then was.

This happened in 1931. Then political ambition tempted Morones, and the CROM lost "class" if not caste by mixing its destinies with those of the *Partido Laborista Mexicano*. Morones' chief assistant since 1921, Vicente Lombardo Toledano, seized this opportunity to set up the *Confederación de Obreros y Campesinos de Mexico* (1933). Lombardo Toledano is an intellectual Marxist who once taught in the University of Mexico City. His new association, faithful to the "workers-peasants" pattern prescribed by Moscow, was short-lived. Another Union was afield which was to attain far wider and more permanent success: the CTM (*Confederación de Trabajadores de Mexico*), which Lombardo Toledano joined, tried to attract to his philocommunist views and finally left. The CTM became the regular working-class Union associated with ORIT (Regional Inter-American Union) and with the CIOSL or International Association of Free Trades Unions.

Meanwhile the Mexican communist movement, under the leadership of Hernán Laborde, made little or no headway in the masses but made some progress among intellectuals. Laborde was then upholding a policy of mass alignment against President Cárdenas. Lombardo Toledano, who was a Cardenist, was called to Moscow in 1935 in time for the VIIth Congress of the Comintern and returned with Popular Front slogans.

At the outbreak of the war, the Communist Party in Mexico was in a delicate position. Not very popular with the masses, though it had attracted not a few intellectuals, it had to struggle both with Trotsky, settled in Mexico in the middle 'thirties, and with the fallacies, inconsistencies and somersaults of Stalin's international policy.

Argentina

Born of a scission of the Socialist Party, led by Victorio Codovilla and Rodolfo Guioldi, the Argentine Communist Party soon benefited from the special attention devoted to it by Moscow. The Party was regularly constituted on 5th-6th January, 1918, in a congress under the chairmanship of José F. Penelón, and one of the communists present, the Chilean Luis E. Recabarren, was said to be Lenin's right-hand man in Latin America. The field, however, was already well ploughed by several rivals, socialists and anarcho-syndicalists, for the strong Spanish and Italian element in the Argentine population is favourable to anarchism. At the First International Latin American Communist Conference (1929), mentioned above, Argentina was represented by fourteen delegates. The Argentine Committee left by the Conference in charge of policy for Argentina was presided over by Miguel Contreras. The Party was not big but it was prosperous and it housed itself with some ease and comfort in the "House of the Proletariat" where it attracted the studious with a library and the less studious with a cinema-hall.

The revolution of 1930 which overthrew the radical government of Hipólito Irigoyen was as opposed to communism as Irigoyen had been, if not favourable, lax and indifferent. The new government searched the House of the Proletariat, and on strength of documents thus unearthed, decided also to search the the seat of the Soviet Commercial Agency. This led to the discovery of the pipeline of secret agents which fed the Argentine Communist Party with money. The party sought to regain popularity and funds by strike agitation. It was outlawed for a year but allowed to return to open political life in 1932.

With the coming of the Popular Front tactics adopted by the VIIth Congress in 1935, the activity of the communist intellectuals increased, since the task now would consist in attracting the middle class sector of political life. The Party set up the AIAPE (*Agrupacion de Intelectuales, Artistas, Periodistas y Escritores*) by no means limited to open and avowed communists, and no doubt able to catch within its nets many a naïve and well-meaning liberal mind of the "why not?" type.

In December 1936, as the outcome of the arrest of the treasurer of the Argentine Communist Party, an official paper laid before a Committee of the Argentine Senate informed the Committee as follows:

1. Communist propaganda in Argentina was directed from Moscow through a special office residing in Paris.

2. Money is received from abroad towards the expenses of this propaganda. It comes through the Paris office.

3. This system extends to neighbouring countries.

4. The communist leaders are subsidized by the Party and money is received from abroad to that end.

Towards 1938, a splinter group left the Communist Party owing to opposition to Stalinism and joined the Trotskyite IVth International. One of its leaders, Mateo Fossa, saw Trotsky in Mexico. At the time, Trotsky saw in Stalin a traitor to the cause of Latin American emancipation (which Trotsky identified with agrarian reform) and put in Stalin's mouth words to this effect. (This is supposed to be Stalin talking to Washington, London and Paris): "Recognize me as partner on terms of equality and I shall help you to crush the revolutionary movement in the colonies and semi-colonies, for to that effect I dispose of hundreds of agents such as Lombardo Toledano."

Thus the Argentine Party reached the outbreak of the war as a relatively unimportant factor in politics, without much mass but with a strong intellectual following, and a somewhat theatrical threat from Trotskyite left wingers.

Chile

The Chilean Communist Party was founded in 1920 by Luis Emilio Recabarren. He had in fact founded it as the Socialist Party of Workers in 1912; but after Lenin's victory, he proposed to his colleagues to go over to communism which was actually done on 1st January, 1922. It was Rodolfo Ghioldi, the Argentine communist, who persuaded those recalcitrant members who preferred to remain "socialists", at any rate in name, to accept the new name as a compulsory condition for admission to the Moscow fellowship.

Recabarren was called to Moscow where he remained from 1922 to 1924. He died soon after his return, in somewhat obscure circumstances, and was succeeded by Manuel Hidalgo. The Chilean Communist Party was strong and influential from its inception, owned five dailies and a number of weeklies, and in the general election of 1926 won two seats in the Senate and seven in the Lower House.

When Carlos Ibañez became President, first by force and then at the polls (1927), he arrested the communist leaders. Official persecution and internal dissensions among the leaders told against the Party during Ibañez's mandate (1927-31). From 1930 on, the party was split between the orthodox branch led by Elias Lafertte and Contreras Labarca and a dissident branch led by Manuel Hidalgo and Humberto Mendoza.

When Ibañez fell, the Hidalgo-Mendoza group organized a Central Committee in opposition to the Lafertte-Contreras Committee, the only one recognized by Moscow. Both groups presented candidates for Parliament and took part in political activities, competing with each other, sometimes violently. Finally, in 1933, the Hidalgo faction joined Trotsky's Fourth International.

Such was the situation when the VIIth Comintern Congress adopted the Popular Front tactics. This change of tactical approach may well have been one of the first cases of Chinese influence in Latin American affairs, for it is asserted* that the Peruvian communist Eudocio Ravines, after a conversation in the neighbourhood of Moscow with Mao Tse-tung, Li Li San and Chu-Teh, identified himself with the new tactics, i.e. the united front of all classes against imperialism and for agrarian reform; and with this new ideological baggage he was sent to Chile to share in the coming presidential struggle, in the company of a number of other communists, a German camouflaged as Manuel Cazón, a Russian who turned his native Kazanov into Casanova, and a Venezuelan, Ricardo Martínez, who was Codovilla's right-hand man. (Ravines has since turned his energies against communism.)

As a result of these events a number of changes took place in the set up of Chilean working-class forces. The Workers

*By Mario Fiorini in an article on communism in Peru, *Estudios sobre el Comunismo*, Santiago de Chile, No. 16, April-June 1957, p. 69.

Federation (*Federacion Obrera de Chile*) led by a communist, Ocampo, and the National Confederation of Legal Syndicates, combined into the National Front of Syndical Unity; and the radical party came to terms with socialists and communists in 1936. This led to the presidential election of 1938 when Pedro Aguirre Cerda was elected by the Popular Front though by a small majority. The outbreak of the war was fatal to this idyll, for radicals and socialists declared in favour of the West and the communists had to follow Stalin's incoherencies.

Peru

The somewhat belated development of communism in Peru is due to the fact that the political area for its growth was occupied by the APRA (*Alianza Popular Revolucionaria Americana*) formed by Victor Raul Haya de la Torre in 1924 shortly after his return from a visit to Russia where he saw Lenin, and to Switzerland where he was well received by Romain Rolland.* The APRA programme incorporated nearly every one of the ingredients which composed communism: the emancipation of workers and peasants, and, therefore, of the Indians; nationalization of industries and redistribution of lands; anti-Americanism and anti-"imperialism". There was but one ingredient missing, by no means easy to advertise: subservience to Moscow. Thus, for many a year the APRA was a serious obstacle to the growth of communism.

Whether the APRA was Marxist or not is a matter for discussion, in which, moreover, its leaders might not be in complete agreement. Haya de la Torre has a mind of his own, and he could discern many a loophole in the somewhat pedantic application of Marxist or even Marxist-Leninist theories, built on a European experience, to the less developed, mixed societies of his continent. His ideology, in fact, conformed rather to what was later to be "discovered" in Moscow under the slogan of

*It was then that I met this attractive young Peruvian idealist, for Romain Rolland wrote to me asking me to intervene, as the Swiss authorities, suspicious of the Bolshevik odour attached to him since his visit to Lenin, were on the point of expelling him. I was glad to be able to ward off the danger.

popular front tactics; with a difference, however, since for him it was a sincere endeavour at a social revolution or swift evolution impelled by a union of all the classes save the privileged possessors of land and capital; while for Moscow it was a mere trick to seize power for the Party.

One of Haya's lieutenants, José Carlos Mariátegui, a gifted printer, self taught, excellent writer and acute thinker, was unconvinced by Haya's views and became the chief Marxist theoretician not only of Peru but of Latin America. He seceded from the APRA in 1928, and founded the Communist Party of Peru in 1929. His prominent companions were Eudocio Ravines, Julio Portocarrero and Fernando Bazán. Mariátegui and Ravines became the men trusted by Moscow, so far as Peru was concerned, and even beyond, as was soon to be shown in the almost decisive intervention of Ravines to establish the Popular Front in Chile and so bring about the election of Aguirre Cerda as President in 1938. Nevertheless, on the eve of the war, the Peruvian Communist Party was by no means strong, and nearly all the revolutionary spirit of the country was being canalized into active politics by the APRA.

Venezuela

Long before the foundation of the Venezuelan Political Party (1931), a Venezuelan communist, Ricardo Martinez, had reached a prominent position in the councils of the Comintern. In 1920, after years of activity against Latin American *Caudillism*, he settled in the U.S.A. and became a member of the American Communist Party. He was soon summoned to Moscow and attended the VIth Congress of the Comintern (1928) and later of the Profintern (Red syndicalist International) where he became Latin American Representative. As such he attended the First Latin American Conference which met in Buenos Aires 1st-12th May 1929, where he explained the peculiarly difficult conditions in which communist activity and propaganda had to be carried out under the fierce dictatorship of Juan Vicente Gómez.

One of the students who had to exile themselves after the

failure of the general strike they had organized in 1928 against the dictator, was Rómulo Betancourt. Another one, Gustavo Machado, founded in exile the Venezuelan Revolutionary Party, and got in touch with Sandino. He later took part in the abortive rebellion against Gómez organized by General Rafael Urbina. In 1931, the Communist Party of Venezuela was born, mostly on paper; though, even so, it was admitted into the Comintern while many of its prominent members were imprisoned and tortured in Venezuela.

Gómez died in 1935, and his successor (and son-in-law), Eliazar López Contreras, began his term of office in a liberalizing mood, which allowed many an exile to return to the country. The National Democratic Party born soon after united most of them, but not for long, for Rómulo Betancourt stood up against all communist influence. The communists left and founded the Party under the two brothers Machado (Eduardo and Gustavo) and Juan Bautista Fuenmayor. Neither of the two parties was able to deploy, for López Contreras, forgetting his short-lived liberalism, persecuted them both with an impartial ruthlessness, so that exile or prison was again the choice among the leaders when the world war broke out.

Brazil

The political, economic and sociological conditions of Brazil towards the early twenties of this century lent themselves to an easy propagation of revolutionary doctrines, for the land workers in the *fazendas* or estates on the one hand, and the urban workers in the dismal outskirts of the big cities on the other, were an easy prey at any rate for the negative, resentful aspects of proletarian propaganda. The political conjuncture was then by no means favourable to a peaceful evolution towards more freedom and comfort for the depressed masses. The President, Arturo da Silva Bernardes, had developed a somewhat dictatorial and imperious style of government which allowed no scope whatsoever for reasonable progress.

Communism was then becoming vocal in nearly every Latin American nation. In Brazil, its leader was to be a young captain, Luiz Carlos Prestes, who was to impart to it a style of his own not unconnected with the old traditions of the country; for his propaganda mission was to partake of the pioneering spirit of the old settlers. He organized a kind of expedition in a para-military style to penetrate deep into the countryside and seek followers among the depressed peasantry working for a pittance on the land (1924).

There was boldness and imagination in the plan; but there was shrewdness as well; for Prestes realized that once far away from the centres of authority, the dictatorial power of the State was bound to slacken; and such bars and bolts as he might find against his mission were more likely to come from local effective forces than from those of the State—forces there-fore which he would be nearly always in a position to counter since he had one of his own, which would allow him a good run before his enterprise came to an end.

The expedition, starting from São Paolo, went first to Iguassú, then turned north until it reached the São Francisco river, then west towards Bolivia. It ran up against the federal army, which Prestes, of course, had no intention of meeting in the field, and was finally broken up. Prestes and a number of his followers took refuge in Argentina; but the stir remained in the land and was felt for many years afterwards. Its memories are not without some influence in whatever power communism —and Prestes—possess in Brazil to this day.

Brazilian delegations were soon active in the communist con-gresses convened in one or other of the cities of the continent. As for Brazil itself, when Getulio Vargas was just beginning to consolidate his hold over the country, the Communist Party tried its hand at a putsch. On 27th November, 1935, red flags were flown in a number of military establishments in Rio de Janeiro, Natal (capital of the State of Rio Grande do Norte) and Recife (capital of the State of Pernambuco). The govern-ment artillery bombarded the rebel headquarters at Afogados, a suburb of Recife; but the stiffest resistance came from the national capital itself, where the cadets of the Air Force were in open rebellion as well as some infantry (the 3rd regiment).

Though suppressed with relative ease, this rising was a straw
in the wind, for it showed how communist propaganda of an
activist and conspiratorial type had penetrated the army.

A second communist rebellion seemed to be ready for the
beginning of October 1937, but it was nipped in the bud by
the government and led to many arrests. How far this event
was determined by the convenience of disposing of all the
powers of a "state of war" to wage a presidential campaign,
it would be difficult to say. At any rate Getulio Vargas was
re-elected (11th November, 1937) and all political parties dissolved (4th December)

Cuba

The Cuban Communist Party was founded between 1923,
when negotiations began, and 1925, when its first congress took
place, by two converging groups, one socialist and the other one
anarcho-syndicalist. It was officially recognized by the IIIrd
International in 1928. Its beginnings were not brilliant, for it
did not find a congenial atmosphere under the dictatorship of
General Gerardo Machado.

Its fortunes began to smile under the first dictatorship of
Batista; for though at first the new dictator frowned at these
rivals whom he found worming their way to power in small
town councils, he later thought it wiser to adopt the Popular
Front policy favoured by Moscow. He therefore allowed the
communists openly to set up (1937) the *Partido de Unión
Revolucionaria,* which was the usual mixture we have so often
observed in other countries whereby the Communist Party
absorbs and dissolves other parties or factions it wants to wipe
out. This time, under the pretext of union against fascism, and
smiled at by Batista, the Cuban communist Führer Juan Marinello, was to preside over the swallowing up by communism of
as many socialist organizations as possible.

Grateful to Batista, the Communist Party declared through
its Central Committee, in July 1938, that the dictator "no
longer was the nucleus of reaction, but the defender of
democracy". The Secretary General of the Party, Blas Roca,

came to an agreement with the dictator, who enabled the Party to come out of its (purely on paper) clandestinity, declaring that it was now "a democratic party which pursues its ends within the framework of the capitalist system and renounces viclence as a political method".

Thus liberated, the Party celebrated its Third Congress in 1939: 347 delegates; 23,300 party members. This congress confirmed the Popular Front policy, mainly in order to back the re-election of Batista in the coming presidential election. The Party began by strengthening its industrial front, securing the appointment of the communist Lázaro Peña as Secretary General of the Unified Syndicates, and infiltrating the whole administration, in particular the Ministry of Labour.

Batista called a Constituent Assembly in 1939, in which the Communists obtained six members; and in the 1940 general election for an ordinary Parliament under the new Constitution, they won ten seats. Juan Marinello was elected for Havana. The communists heartily voted for Batista's re-election, and Juan Marinello and his fellow communist Carlos Rafael Rodriguez accepted to serve in his cabinet.

6. — THE WAR AND AFTER

During the Second World War, the Communist Parties in Latin America faithfully followed the vagaries of Stalin's *Realpolitik*. It was not always easy and they often lost face— and body as well. When Hitler attacked the Soviet Union, the communists crossed the line and from sworn enemies of the United States and her "imperialism", they became her friends and the defenders of democracy by her side. This did not prevent them from getting into trouble in some cases immediately after the war, as for instance in Brazil, where President Dutra declared them illegal in 1946.

Since the war, the Soviet organization for Latin America seems to be constituted along the following lines:

1. The sixth section of the Foreign Secretariat of the Central Committee of the Soviet Union Communist Party;

2. G.U.J.A., i.e. Chief Directorate for South America. It is composed of two autonomous organisms: The Research Consultative College and the Aid Office for South American Republics. The first acts as the information and technical adviser of the second.

These two organisms are in their turn affiliated to the Marx-Engels-Lenin Institute. The Communist Office for Latin America working from Mexico, was transfigured (May 1955) into the *Junta Suprema de la Libertad Latinoamericana* (code name CIUDAD). Most of its members are foreign to Latin America, and only a handful are Latin American, Spanish or Portuguese. There is also a *Junta Revolucionaria del Caribe*. The head of these organizations and of their three components, *Junta del Pacifico, Junta del Atlantico* and *Junta Revolucionaria,* is a Soviet officer with a Mexican passport and a Spanish name, Pablo Jiménez, who during the Spanish Civil war was an A.D.C. to the communist general "Walter". He was also instructor for anti-imperialist action in Prague and Imre Münich's collaborator in Hungary.

Münich was vice-president of the Economic and Social Commission, an organism which, under cover of a somewhat neutral title, was busy with anti-American activities in Latin America. Its President was a Rumanian, Mihail Broila. This Commission was set up in Moscow in 1952, the year in which another similar organization was born, the Committee of Cooperation for the Development of International Trade, on which sat representatives of the Communist Parties of Argentina, Brazil and Guatemala.

At that time, at any rate, the general opinion among Moscow leaders seems to have been that there was no immediate prospect of communist victories, i.e. seizures of political power, in any American country. The tactical activity of the local communist parties was directed towards the disintegration of the national life of the country concerned and the exploitation of the ill feeling thus created to feed campaigns against the United States.

The next line of Soviet organization is the diplomatic and

consular establishment of the Soviet Union and other communist countries. Latin American nations have by no means been the first to grant recognition to the Soviet Union, nor have they been remiss in breaking relations with her now and then. They found no particular guidance on the part of the United States in this respect. It is not to be wondered at then if, disposing as it did of the Soviet Union Embassies and of the Embassies and Legations of the European satellites, the World Communist Party was able to organize its infiltration into the body politic of Latin America. Its chief fields of development were the political, the commercial and the cultural.

According to official American information for 1958 the total membership of the Communist Party for the twenty republics was about 209,000 to 229,000, an increase of 5% on the previous year. Every form of propaganda was on the increase, publications being more numerous and of better quality. As for radio broadcasts, they increased to 104 hours 25 minutes per week. One of the most attractive of these measures of propaganda, free travel to the Soviet Union, was also on the increase, 1,200 persons having been invited, an increase of 100 over 1956 (1957 was exceptional owing to a Youth congress that took place in Moscow). As for trade, it was estimated at 240 to 250 million dollars, an increase of 20%, Soviet Union and satellites included.

The Party was legally allowed to exist in Argentina, Bolivia, Chile, Colombia, Ecuador, Mexico, Uruguay and Venezzuela; its percentage of votes was nowhere higher than 6% (Venezuela) except in Chile where it reached 29%, though in coalition with the left socialists, in the November 1958 presidential elections.

Some measure of the liveliness of the so-called cultural penetration of the World Communist Party into Latin America may be gathered from the fact that in 1958 the number of associations known as "binational", purporting to "bring together" the culture of a given Latin American nation and that of the Soviet Union or a satellite, was 84, not counting five Yugoslav ones. Some of these associations have branches in provincial cities. For instance, the Argentine-Soviet Institute of Cultural Relations is active in seventeen cities.*

The 1958 catalogue of the EPU (*Ediciones Pueblos Unidos*), a communist publishing house centred in Uruguay, contained close upon 1,200 titles of communist books circulating in Latin America, either published by EPU itself or by other houses, Soviet or of other nations. In my personal experience, Soviet or pro-Soviet books are omnipresent in the continent, pamphlets abundant and the communist pressure is so keen that it turns up where least expected, as for instance in books for children.

There were in 1958 over one hundred Soviet and Chinese papers in circulation in Latin America, including those openly published by the diplomatic missions. They are printed in Spanish, Portuguese, French and other languages. Over and above these official publications, over three hundred communist dailies and weeklies were appearing regularly: and two Soviet publications were being printed in Buenos Aires: *Soviet Literature* and *Problems of Peace and Socialism*. The number of publishing houses and bookshops publishing communist material was estimated at over one hundred.

7.—THE TRADE DRIVE

As for trade, the group of the Soviet Union and satellites starts from a modest basis. Its total foreign trade stands at hardly more than 3% of the total world trade. In 1956, the non-communist world had bought from the communist goods to the value of $2,910 million, of which $1,948 million had been bought by Europe. Alongside these figures, the share of Latin America was modest: $146 million. Nevertheless, the Soviet Union fully realized the political and possibly strategic value of such a trade even before the Cuban revolution.

*Buenos Aires, Belén, Blanca, Córdoba, Cruz del Eje, Mar del Plata, Mendoza, Paraná, Posadas, Presidente Roque Saenz Peña, Rosario, San Francisco, Sante Fe, Santiago del Estero, Tandil, Tucumán and Villa María.

The Soviet plan comprises: (*a*) credits; (*b*) technical aid; (c) bilateral trade agreements; (d) commercial penetration. The plan is evidently aimed at loosening the ties that bind the Southern to the Northern part of the continent: but it would be a mistake to imagine that such an aim in itself would be repellent to the South. The chances are that the pro-Soviet part of the South would accept it with alacrity because it came from Moscow, and most of the anti-Soviet sector with as much alacrity in spite of its coming from Moscow.

A deliberate effort was made on the occasion of President Frondizi's inauguration (1st May, 1958), when the Soviet special representative, Mr Tarasov, Vice-President of the Supreme Soviet, was accompanied by the First Deputy Minister of Foreign Affairs, Mr Kuznetsov; this latter also visited Uruguay and Mexico. The tendentious, non-strictly commercial nature of this activity is shown by the offers to buy surplus stocks of copper, tin, coffee, sugar, at higher prices than those prevailing at the time. These offers are made with a concrete and accurate knowledge of the needs of the country concerned. Thus, the Soviet-Brazilian commercial agreement of 9th December 1959 stipulated exchanges worth on either side $27 million in 1960, $37 million in 1961 and $45 million in 1962. The Soviet Union was to supply Brazil with oil (the country's biggest consumer of dollars) as well as machinery, metals and chemicals, in exchange for $18 million worth of coffee in 1960 as well as other exports such as beans, vegetable oils and hides.

The Tarasov-Kuznetsov visit of May 1958 to Argentina bore fruit on 27th October of the same year, when a trade agreement was signed in Moscow. Here was a case in which the short-sighted policy of the United States forced a Latin American country to cross the line. The *Yacimientos Petrolíferos Federales* (YPF), the Argentine autonomous (State) organization for the exploitation of the national petrol, unable to find help in the U.S.A. owing to American bigotry about private enterprise, obtained under this agreement with the Soviet Union a credit of $100 million to secure oil equipment in Russia, at $2\frac{1}{2}\%$ per annum. Several minor though still important agreements were also signed, providing, for instance, for delivery of Russian road-making machinery.

On 18th-28th November, 1958, Vice-President Mikoyan visited Mexico and spoke on the advisability of developing all kinds of relations between the two countries. He had a reception which was polite but cool in official circles, but much warmer among intellectuals and students.

Similar moves are observable in other countries. A Soviet trade bureau has been opened in Montevideo. The Soviet Union offers to buy Uruguayan wool to pay for oil. Offers of Soviet industrial equipment are being studied in Colombia, El Salvador, Mexico, Panama. Chile endeavours to sell her copper. Bolivia complains that Soviet tin policy, which consists in dumping it at cheap prices on the western market (possibly to punish Malaya and Indonesia for their insubordination) is producing disastrous effects on her none too healthy economy. Other warning voices are heard, and cautious attitudes noted; but all in all, the commercial penetration of the Soviet Union in South America is impressive.

8. — A FEW TYPICAL SITUATIONS

Mexico

The membership of the Party is estimated at 100,000. Its Secretary General is Dionisio Encinas, of peasant origin. This, however, only applies to the PCM (*Partido Comunista Mexicano*) recognized by Moscow. There is a splinter group, *Partido Obrero y Campesino de Mexico,* led by an ex-railway-man, Valentin Campa, who used to be one of the official Party leaders, but was expelled on orders from Moscow because of his insubordination to Moscow's man in the country, Vicente Lombardo Toledano.

The Mexican law about parties is by no means simple; the way it is applied is less simple still. Lombardo Toledano is in fact the leader of a party, *Partido Popular,* which is the only one officially recognized of the three in Mexico, although not mustering the minimum of 75,000 members the law demands to be admitted as a "national party". This is the somewhat picturesque set up of the communist political life of Mexico at the present time.

This political life of communism in Mexico is not easy. The peculiar way in which communist parties are led, and in particular the one-man-show character they are prone to take, is not suited to the Latin American character. Lombardo Toledano is too much of a monopolist of power, and of some of its most coveted plums such as frequent trips to Russia and to China, to please his companions; his directives are too often inspired in the interests of the Soviet Union to appeal to the intellectuals of one of the most nationalistic countries in the world.

In Parliament, the communists have lost the little membership they had. In industrial life, they control very few unions. Lombardo Toledano, in control of the CTM (*Confederación de Trabajadores de Mexico*), founded the CTAL (*Confederación de Trabajadores de América Latina*) which he intended to channel into Soviet waters. It lasted for as long as it took the component national Unions to become aware of his intention.

Nevertheless, though its political and industrial set-up is not impressive, communism wields a real power in Mexico. The most impressive manifestation of this power will be found in the press and similar organs of public opinion. A number of periodicals are published by the several communist political organizations, either openly, such as *La Voz de Mexico* or *Problemas de America Latina,* or in a camouflaged form, no less efficient under their masks. Moreover, there are newspapers by no means of the communist observance whose supplements are in the hands of fellow-travellers.

There is a strong communist influence in the university where a number of key posts are in the hands of communists or fellow-travellers; and the biggest of Mexican publishing houses, *Fondo de Cultura Económica,* erected with State funds and to this day subsidized to the tune of 600 million Mexican pesos, is led by an Argentine fellow-traveller, Arnaldo Orfila. A number of other publishing houses are also under communist or fellow-traveller leadership. Communists too are the artists who control the *Comisión Nacional de Artes Plásticas*, a fact which enables them to win over many an artist in a country in which the State is by far the most active and powerful Maecenas.

All this activity is directed and controlled by a Soviet Embassy, comprising no less than 350, perhaps as many as 400 persons, let alone their colleagues who work in the Polish and Czech Legations. Their activities are multifarious and no doubt many of them nefarious, as was revealed by some ugly incidents which occurred in 1957 in Guadalajara (9th May) and later in Morelia and in Mexico City. These turbulent events were traced back to Soviet agents, respectively Nicolai Trujimov and Yuri Nicolaievich Paparov. There is a second centre of similar activities at the Soviet Embassy in Montevideo.

The general picture is therefore somewhat patchy. The provincial attempts at disorder led by Soviet agents are mere stunts; and the impressive scene in the capital may seem perhaps merely literary. Yet communism in Mexico is a real threat. The country, despite its federal constitution on paper is centralistic almost to a monarchical extent. The capital is the true political motor of the nation, and the amalgam of nation, State, government, executive, civil service, intelligentsia, journalism, radio and public opinion in one single relatively small *élite* renders the nation liable to a sudden change if such a change were to take place in this *élite*—if, for instance, a forceful President came to be elected animated by strong pro-Soviet feeling.

Argentina

The Communist Party stood against Perón on the basis of the National Front tactics then orthodox in Moscow, drew nearer to the dictator as soon as he inaugurated a policy of agreement with the Soviet Union, and went back to irate opposition after the visit of Mr Milton Eisenhower to Perón in 1953. All this accords with the usual steps and counter-steps of communist minuetti conducted from Moscow.

During the honeymoon with Perón the communists did their best to increase their hold on the country and to infiltrate into the press, civil service, army and banks, backed by the Soviet Ambassador, Grigori Rezhanov, who was on the best of terms with the dictator. The party was doubly led: on the surface, by its public organization; and underground, by the group *"Atención"* which had been organized in 1943 by the Spanish Communist Sebastián Zapirain, alias Julio Lafage. Led at first by Rodolfo Ghioldi from Uruguay and by Victorio Codovilla from Chile, *Atención* was later transferred to Bahía Blanca, but in 1949, on the strength of Perón's friendship for communism, to Buenos Aires itself. Its leaders had been trained in USSR (4), Czechoslovakia (2), Uruguay (7) and Mexico (11).

A special effort seems to have been made at that time to acquire information on Argentine military establishments, led from the Latin American Communist office in Mexico (code name: CIUDAD) under Julio López, represented in Mexico by Diego Alonso, and by the Soviet Embassy in Buenos Aires. The aim seems to have been less international than national, i.e. to secure control of the armed forces, by-passing the regular officers, and to that effect, to establish communist cells in the units. This action was made easier by a similar disintegrating effort made in Perón's interest by the dictator's minister of war.

At Perón's fall the Communist Party was foremost among the forces that fought against the Aramburu government in its efforts to give back their freedom to the trades unions. The communists insisted on preserving the strong centralization of the working-class syndicates introduced by Perón on the Fascist-Franco model; and they adopted a political programme identical with that for which the present President, Frondizi, then stood, notably a political amnesty (which then meant liberation of imprisoned Peronists), no Prebisch plan for the restoration of the country's economy (which meant economic chaos) and an international "peace policy" (which meant a pro-Soviet alignment).

Dr Frondizi was then a member of the International Red Aid and would come out on the communist side in this or that public controversy. His brother, Silvio Frondizi, is one of the leaders of *Praxis*, a group of intellectuals well known for their extremist left-wing views. It is well known that Dr Frondizi secured his election through pacts with communists and Peronists, so that when Perón made public his support of Dr Frondizi, the communists announced that they would vote for him also.

In spite of this unprincipled path, or possibly because of it, the communists have gained popular support almost continuously: 71,000 votes in 1951; 89,000 in 1954; 192,000 in 1958. It is not yet spectacular for a 10 million electorate, but might soon become a not inconsiderable parliamentary force, the more so as it is perhaps the richest party in the nation. It keeps a daily, *La Hora*, with a circulation estimated at 10,000 and a weekly, *Nuestra Palabra*, with about the same circulation; a monthly, *Nueva Era*, the spokesman of the Central Committee, and a daily, *Nuestra Tierra*, which is meant to arouse the countryside, where Party agents are very active. It also publishes *Juventud* with a 25,000 circulation, *Nuestras Mujeres* for the women, and *Unidad Sindical* (60,000) for the trades unions. It runs a Movement for the Democratization and Independence of Trades Unions which acts in exactly the opposite direction to what its name suggests; for there is no doubt that the continued centralization of the Union system imposed on President Frondizi by his own pacts with communists and Peronists is undemocratic and contrary to the independence of the Unions, and has been one of the thorns in the flesh of the President himself after his courageous and public-spirited abjuration of the errors of his candidacy.

Politically, the Party is not a first-rate force; but conspiratorially it is. Its hold on the intellectuals and on the professional classes increases daily, and it infiltrates at all stages in the administrative and cultural life of the nation, let alone the Unions Movement.

On 25th September, 1958, the Argentine police discovered in a suburban mansion, "Stella Maris", of Buenos Aires a school for the training of sabotage and rebel leaders. It was discreetly hidden under leafy trees. There were nineteen men and five women in training under a teacher, Alberto Ferrari. It was the Latin American School of Instruction for the Communist Party Cadres. The students were mostly Argentines, but there were also a number of other Latin American nationalities represented, as well as Spaniards and Italians. The running of the school cost 40,000 Argentine pesos a month. The students were only allowed out two together. The organization was military. A number of students of this school were later arrested in the course of riots in Buenos Aires.

The government had to react, and a number of measures were taken against the communist press, communist diplomats found too zealous and even the Communist Party, whose banishment was considered in 1959. The situation remains delicate both on the political and on the economic front. The true remedy would, of course, lie in a stabilization of the economic and political life of the country, since its inherent wealth would do the rest. But this defines a vicious circle which only time can break.

Chile

This is the Latin American country in which communism has the strongest political position, measured in popular votes and also with regard to its alliances with other parties. The FRAP is exactly the kind of political contraption that has enabled the Party in other cases—such as that of Prague—to conquer power and kick away the socialist ladder it had used for its ascent. The Fierlinger is at hand. His name is Salvador Allende.

Nevertheless, triumph is not yet round the corner. On 3rd April, 1960, municipal elections were held in the whole country. There is a yardstick for judging the result, i.e. the 1947 general election, when the Communist Party obtained 13.8% of the votes. This time, the communist vote was no more than 6.39% and the number of councillors elected, 82, as against 120 that went to their allies, the socialists. All in all, the whole FRAP obtained 265,000 votes, a loss of 89,000 on the results of the 1958 presidential election.

More recent tests tell a different story. The progress made in the public opinion of the country by the two allied parties of the left was forcibly brought to the fore in the 1961 general election for Parliament (5th March). The whole Lower Chamber (147 members) and 25 out of 45 Senators were to be elected. While the contingent of the three government parties (Radicals, Liberals and Conservatives) fell from 97 to 84 in the Lower House, the combined strength of socialists and communists rose from 14 to 28 (15 c. plus 13 s.). Furthermore, out of the 25 new Senators, five are communists and four socialists.

There seems to be a certain tension between the two allied parties owing to the reluctance of the Communist Party to sacrifice some local electoral interests to guarantee the re-election (in 1961) of the socialist leader, Salvador Allende. On the other hand, the CUT (*Central Unica de Trabajadores*), by far the most important Trades Union confederation seems to have become a communist-controlled agency for penetration into the Unions. Its president, Clotario Blest, calls himself a social-Christian, but is generally considered as subservient to communist interests.

Blest was the chief, and the most violent, speaker at an open-air meeting which took place in Santiago on 3rd November, 1960, in which he incited the people to revolt against the austerity measures of President Alessandri, dictated though they were by his anxiety to arrest inflation. Disorders ensued, and a brush with the police which caused two deaths and wounded forty. On the occasion of the funeral of the dead (7th November), fresh disorders were provoked by the communists and shouts of "Down with Yankee Imperialism" were heard. Blest was imprisoned.

Blest is also the President of the National Movement of Solidarity with, and Defence of, the Cuban Revolution, many of whose leading members are communists. Cuba is filling Chile with propaganda, and its new agency, *Prensa Latina*, is most active, while about 500 Chileans have visited Cuba at the invitation of Castro's government.

Communist action in the countryside is carried out through the ANACH (*Asociacion Nacional de Agricultores de Chile*), composed of small landowners and farmers, and the *Federación Nacional de Trabajadores Agricolas*, composed of land workers, led by the land-adviser to the CUT, César Escobar Cuevas. The movement is served by a paper *El Surco* (The Furrow). It is worth while to point out that the opponents of communism recognize that the near triumph of the FRAP in the 1958 presidential election was due to the fact that the peasant vote was allured by promises of an agrarian reform on the Bolivian model. The FRAP candidate, Allende, had an *Agrarian Reform Draft Bill* widely distributed as a pamphlet. The result was an undoubted majority for him in most rural areas. In the XIth National Congress of the Party (18th-23rd November, 1958) an alliance of the peasants and the proletarians was declared to be the immediate aim of the Party.

The present Secretary General of the Party, Luis Corvalán, outlined the action of communism in Latin America at the plenary session of the Central Committee (10th May, 1959). He spoke in terms which already reveal a certain Chinese influence —an influence he did not hide, for he had recently discussed matters with Mao Tse-tung. His attitude was contrary to the Latin American Common Market, a typically communist attitude similar to that of the Soviet Union's systematic opposition to any federation of Eastern European countries after the Second World War.

There is a movement of opposition to the communist influence over the Trades Unions. It works through the *Central de Fuerzas del Trabajo* organized by an ex-communist leader, Victor Labbé Diaz. It is doubtful whether this movement will be able to struggle against the richest and one of the best led parties in the country. Furthermore, the intellectual exchanges between Chile on the one hand and Soviet Russia and China on the other are most lively; travelling to and fro being almost continuous. University men, sporting teams, ballets and operas come and go; and there are an influential daily and many weeklies and the usual youth, and women, and what-not associations.

The *élite* is caught in the movement. And the political set-up lends itself, perhaps better than anywhere else, to a surprise seizure of power. The Army looks on.

9. — ENTER CHINA

On 15th September, 1951, the Chilean poet Pablo Neruda* landed on Peking airfield in the company of Ilya Ehrenburg and two other communists. He came from Moscow. At the beginning of October 1952 a Conference of Peace Defenders was convened in Peking, which devoted special attention to the Pacific. The Latin American delegates (eleven countries) declared for closer ties between their continent and China. A Contact Committee was appointed, of which Neruda was elected one of the vice-presidents.

In 1953 Mao Tse-tung issued instructions to the Chinese Communist Party pointing to the importance of Latin America for isolating the United States. In 1956 the Peking Opera toured Latin America. In 1958 Radio Peking started broadcasting seven to fourteen hours weekly in Spanish and seven in Portuguese. These broadcasts are competent. In March 1959 a meeting was held in Peking attended by representatives of the Latin American Communist Parties in the presence of Mao Tse-tung, Liu Shao-shi and Chou En-lai. The parties agreed to spread in their countries Marxist literature prepared in Peking. This was confirmed in October 1959 in Buenos Aires by a meeting of representatives of the principal communist and philo-communist publishing houses (Lautaro, Futuro, Platina, Cartago, Palestra). Platina soon published the works of Mao Tse-tung in two volumes (they were sold out almost at once) and a History of Contemporary China since the Opium War. Cartago published *The Philosophy of Freedom* by the Japanese communist Kenjuro Yanagida; and Palestra, Fidel Castro's speeches under the title of *The Cuban Revolution*.

There exist at present at least eighteen binational associa-

*Real name: Neftalí Reyes.

tions of friendship between China and Latin American nations, notably in Argentina, Brazil, Chile, Mexico and Uruguay.

On 25th May, 1959, a group of Chinese journalists arrived in Uruguay, some from China, some from Cuba, where they were settled as representatives of the New Chinese Agency. One of them, Hau Shi, is the head of the Latin American Department of the People's Paper. They insisted on the formation of an Afro-Asian-Latin-American Front. On the tenth anniversary of the foundation of the Chinese People's Republic, 135 Latin Americans from nineteen countries attended the celebrations as guests. In 1959, 402 Latin Americans were invited in all. These visitors were impressed by the excellent Spanish spoken by their guides. In November 1959, the Chinese began negotiations with a view to establishing in São Paolo an office for the development of trade with the whole of Latin America, though they intended to open branches in Montevideo and Buenos Aires as well.

On 10th May, 1960, Chou En-lai in a declaration to the press conceived in a strong anti-U.S. vein asserted both directly and by implication Chinese interest in Latin America. On 19th April a campaign of "friendship towards Latin America" was launched in Peking at a great assembly attended by 10,000 persons in the presence of Chou En-lai and the Foreign Secretary Chen Yi. The Foreign Secretary and the Mayor of Peking, Peng Chen, received the Latin American visitors, mostly student delegates and artists from a number of countries. Messages were sent to the Latin American youth by the Chinese youth and to the Latin American women by the Chinese women, assuring them that they would be backed "in their rightful struggle" against American "imperialism, cruel abuse and shameful intervention".

What does all this amount to? Are we in the presence of friendly agreement to let Latin America be penetrated by China, a kind of Pope Alexander VI division of the New World into Spanish and Portuguese zones, as some observers claim took place in 1953? Or should we be content with seeing in it merely an assertion of independence on the part of China, an affirmation of her right to spread communism on her own terms? The second solution seems likely to be correct. Some Latin American observers see a certain parallelism between the sociological conditions prevailing in China and those in Latin America* and would quote Mao Tse-tung to outline a profile of Dr Frondizi as the theoretician of the bourgeois-democratic revolution which must (according to Mao Tse-tung) precede the socialist revolution. Furthermore, there are about 100,000 Chinese in Latin America, whose attitude and feelings on these matters it would be rash to try to guess. All in all, a Chinese claim for a share, and not a small one, in the communist action on South America seems to rest on solid foundations.†

10.—CUBA AND AFTER

The general outline of the Cuban revolution is now beginning to emerge as a middle-class protest against Batista led first by Castro towards liberal democracy and then betrayed by him to communism. The outward signs of this betrayal were the dropping of President Urrutia; the sacrifice of two of Castro's comrades in arms, Major Cienfuegos and Major Hubert Matos; the practical replacement of the Sierra Maestra army by a communist militia; and the elimination of the men who, like Señor Miró Cardona, had been the guarantors of the liberal spirit of his movement.

The somewhat belated conversion of Cuba's official communists to *fidelismo* must have resulted from their conviction that Fidel Castro was for them the way to power. A good observer believes that this move must have taken place early in

*See Carlos Montes in *Estudios sobre el Comunismo*, No. 17, p. 119, on a parallel with Argentina.

†I am indebted to Professor Alberto Falcionelli for his paper on Russo-Chinese relations after Stalin's death, read at the Third International Sovietological Conference, Tokyo, 18th-25th Sept., 1960, and to the China Quarterly for proofs of an article by Victor Alba on "The Chinese in Latin America".

1958 after a struggle between the old-Stalinist tendency of Blas Roca, the Secretary General, and a more flexible fraction led by Carlos Rafael Rodriguez.* As late as February 1960, Blas Roca was still speaking about comrades who thought that the revolution was "alien to them"; and on 8th July, 1960 he was still harping on "supporting the government and strengthening the unity of the Party". As the men of the Party are by now deeply entrenched in the administration and the army, the issue is academic.

What matters is that, by now, Cuba has become an ideal bridgehead for communism in the New World. The revolutionary government has broken all relations with the inter-American system, and has concluded a set of agreements, cultural, commercial and political, which amount to her accession to the communist block. The Democratic Revolutionary Front, in a a document submitted to the OAS on 14th November, 1960 asserts that there are now in Cuba numerous communist agents [coming from Russia and China] who occupy key posts in the State; that armaments coming from the Soviet block are being piled up in big quantities, and that the armies fighting against the Cuban people, who oppose Castro, are mostly composed of Russian, Czech and Chinese communists.

As a comment on this aspect of the matter, it is pointed out that the present Soviet ambassador to Cuba, Serge Mihailovich Kudriavtsev, was first secretary of the Soviet Embassy in Canada when in 1946 Igor Guzenko, a civil servant in the code department of the Embassy, "chose liberty" and sought refuge in Canada, where it was found that Kudriavtsev was in fact the chief Soviet spy in Canada.

Add to all this that, of the 100,000 or so Chinese who live in Latin America, about one third live in Cuba, 12,000 of them in Havana. The new régime broke relations with Nationalist China and promptly recognized the Chinese People's Republic (2nd September, 1960). The Chinese residents in Cuba are organized in a League for the New Democracy,

*Theodore Draper, *loc. cit.*

12

a communist body, and the three papers in Chinese which appeared in the Island have become communist. Dr Ernesto ("Che") Guevara has visited China and a trade agreement on the basis of a loan was negotiated as the outcome of a previous visit of Lu Hsu-chang, Chinese deputy minister of Foreign Trade, to Havana on 23rd July, 1960.

It would be hard to exaggerate the importance of these facts. There is a danger that too much stress may be laid on their strategic importance from the hot-war point of view, owing to Cuba's closeness to Florida and to the Panama Canal. The strategic importance of Cuba is far greater from the cold-war than from the hot-war point of view. Cuba is a living example of a Latin American republic that turns her back on the United States; of a people that rebels against the old established bourgeoisie. If the evolution of Cuba is seen accurately, as a fall to the status of a satellite, it may still exert a salutary influence on the continent; if she returns to democracy, purged of her old political corruption, she may save the continent. For the time being she is the base for a second revolutionary communist leap forward which might be fatal for the New World.

At this point, events overtook our narrative. The Cuban liberating expedition was attempted and failed. Whereupon, a chorus of vituperation of the U.S.A. drowned the event. This chorus was by no means harmonious. Close observation allowed the detached hearer to detect within it a number of different strains.

First, a condemnation of all forms and kinds of intervention in the internal affairs of any country by any other country or group of them, amounting to a proclamation of non-intervention as an international dogma. This is a curious stand; for as a matter of fact non-intervention

(*a*) has never been practised;

(*b*) cannot be practised;

(*c*) and would be a most retrograde policy if it could be practised.

(a) *Has never been practised.* This is a matter of fact, and need not be backed by examples. Whenever a nation has been able to intervene in such affairs of another nation as in some way or other concerned her, she has done so. Sometimes the intervening nation was right; sometimes wrong. But the fact of intervention is undeniable throughout history.

(b) *Cannot be practised.* Nations intervene in each other's affairs whether they do so by intervention or by non-intervention. For instance, when Britain and France decided not to intervene in the Spanish Civil War, they did intervene, since their "non-intervention" became one of the chief features of that war, and so shaped it that it was precisely this Anglo-French non-intervention which made inevitable the victory of either the one or the other extreme, the fascist or the communist, and therefore determined the defeat of the western ideology of liberal democracy in the Peninsula.

(c) *Would be a most retrograde policy if it could be practised.* Because the world is fast becoming one, and we are all members of each other. This, by the way, disposes of the plea of *internal affairs* raised for instance by the South African Republic in the case of *apartheid*. There are fewer and fewer affairs nowadays which can be deemed to be internal. Practically everything is, or can become, of world-wide import.

The issue therefore is not whether intervention in itself is right or wrong, since no such issue exists *a priori*; but whether the way it is applied in a given specific case is right or wrong.

The second strain observable within the chorus of vituperation of the U.S.A. on the Cuban occasion was that intervention in this case by the Cuban exiles was wrong because Castro and the Cuban people are right. This is a curious aberration. The issue for us is plain. We, the West, cannot accept systems in which reforms are forced down the gullet of a people by gagging the press and shooting all opponents. That such reforms were overdue is no argument, since it is plain that they would have been carried out by the revolution that brought Castro to power and which he betrayed. He violated his promises and delivered his country to communism. This cannot be gainsaid. Indeed, his later evolution reveals already on his part all the signs of the typical communist behaviour. He has begun to grovel in the usual self-accusations and fulsome praise of the wisdom of the Communist Party; and, in accordance with the usual cynicism of communist policy, he had come to recognize a friend in Trujillo. When certain organs of the free world press still endeavour to shield Castro, they cover one of the most repulsive attitudes the modern world has now and then to witness, one which Castro shares with Sekou Touré and other such leaders: that of a country just born or reborn to freedom embracing as an ally the butcher of the freedom of half a continent. Is not that in itself a proof that the Cuban revolution has strayed from the right path?

Therefore, a Cuban intervention in Cuba was fully justified insofar as its purpose was to re-direct the revolution to its first, ante-dictatorial, liberal-democratic path.

The third strain of vituperation consisted in declaring that the U.S.A. should not have given aid to the Cuban exiles. It is hard to follow the reasoning behind this claim. If, as we have established, the Cuban exiles were right and Castro wrong, why should the American State abstain from an operation which would deliver the continent from the dangers of totalitarianism?

True the United States has a bad record. True she has never reacted against other forms of oppression, indeed has too often favoured them. But a good deed is a good deed for all that, and after all, the administration is new and led by a new leader. All the West can ask is that the invader be not polluted by admitting within its ranks people or parties which collaborated with Batista (unlike Castro who works hand in glove with the Communist Party which collaborated with Batista); and that the American government prove their sincerity by ousting the Trujillo clique immediately after Castro has been ousted.

The fourth strain of vituperation condemns the failure of the expedition. This splits into two sub-strains: one bears on the inefficiency of the attackers. This inefficiency was shocking. It should be digested and remedied for the future. But it is in a way irrelevant. The other is about the union of the defenders. We are assured that "the peasants" were at heart with the militia, and fought together. What else could they do?

How much would it matter if they did? The fact is that Cuba is a totalitarian country, that everybody in the country is therefore immersed in prefabricated opinion, and if not, at any rate, in prefabricated behaviour; and that all arguments on "the Cuban people being behind Castro" are utterly worthless since there is no free, spontaneous, informed public opinion in Cuba.

Conclusion

We are led to conclude that Cuba must be liberated, and that, since it is by now stuffed with communist weapons and technicians, it can only be liberated by the OAS. The argument that Castro had better be left alone and given enough rope to hang himself is worthless. The experience of other nations fallen into the unscrupulous hands of the Communist Party allows of no such optimism. Time could only make of Cuba an impregnable base for communism to spread all over America. The Latin American governments who shilly-shally over it are only preparing the rope with which they will be hanged. Castro must go soon.

But the U.S.A. cannot lead such an operation in the undignified, shamefaced, hidden manner in which the April operation was carried out. It savours too much of a bad conscience. The U.S.A. must act in the light of day. For that she should first purify herself. The occasion is propitious: a new administration, a new President. There must be a clear call from Washington in the style of that superb inaugural speech. Let the Monroe Doctrine be buried, since it is dead. But let the Kennedy Doctrine live. It was put to the world in his inaugural speech. It spelt Freedom. Let the Doctrine of Freedom be proclaimed from the White House,* and, armed with that Doctrine, let the United States lead a spirited operation against

*This was done by President Kennedy in his message to Congress on 26th May.

all dictators—right and left. Other American nations may join in the crusade. *But it must be a crusade.**

*Half at least of the obstacles in the way of an intervention are due to the mistrust with which the United States is still regarded south of the Mexican frontier, a mistrust the advent of Kennedy has, as yet, been unable to dispel. Indeed, it is rumoured that behind the public professions and even actions, such as the Alliance for Progress, excellent though they are in intention, the old financial and business stranglehold remains unimpaired. Thus the meeting of the OAS in Washington (25th October, 1961) was unable to agree on action in Cuba and could do no more than achieve a compromise solution consisting in keeping the idea open. This was done in spite of strong opposition from Argentina and Brazil, adamant against any move contrary to the present Cuban régime. Though in this case the attitude of the two South American nations may have been due less to their distrust of U.S.A. than to their own fears of communism at home.

V

ACTION

I. — A CHANGE OF MIND

L E T us now lift our eyes from the details and look at the whole afresh. The danger is instant; but that is no reason why we should try to rush to avert it with hurried and ill-conceived schemes. Furthermore, an order of urgencies should be clearly thought out. This implies a criterion or yardstick, which, however, is not hard to define. The Latin American problem has been studied within the framework of the world problem; and in this perspective, what has stood out as the chief feature, the first priority of all, is the restoration of the moral authority of the West and above all of the United States.

This is then the first and most ugent task from the paramount point of view of the world as a whole. It turns out to be the first task also from the point of view of the Latin American problem; for it stands to reason that no measure, however well meant and well conceived, can achieve full results while the present mistrust of U.S. motives, and resentment for the past (indeed, present) practices lingers in the South.

In fine, the change of attitude advocated amounts to one of perspective. The U.S.A. has been used to consider Latin American problems as they concern the U.S.A. This is normal and healthy for any ordinary nation to do. It is not so for the U.S.A. because the U.S.A. is not an ordinary nation. World responsibilities have been laid on her, and she must discharge them. This means that she must rise above the national level in most matters of world concern. Therefore she must effect a kind of Copernican conversion of her attitude; no longer considering the other nations as revolving round her, but seeing in them planets revolving round themselves. The U.S.A. is now required by the historical conjuncture to initiate an era of self-denial.*

This remains actual even after the two chief events of the year in the Latin American field: the setting up of the Inter-American Social Progress Trust (27th May, 1961) as the instrument to carry out President Kennedy's Alliance for Progress programme, with its sequel, the Montevideo Inter-American Economic Conference (15th July, 1961); and Mr Adlai Stevenson's visit to a number of Latin American capitals in June 1961. It is significant, by the way, of the plight of the U.S.A. in her dealings with the South that no first-rank statesman could be found for this visit who knew Spanish. Admirable as the choice was in many ways, in fact, the best that could have been made, the efficiency of the tour was certainly reduced by the fact that Mr Stevenson does not know Spanish. Some day perhaps American public men will realize that half the continent speaks another language than English.

As for the Alliance for Progress, though in its spirit and general direction it stands definitely in advance of previous similar plans, the mere gift of six hundred million dollars, though better and more intelligently administered than of old, will not suffice to meet the danger. Something more profound if less spectacular is required. This was already shown in the Montevideo assembly where, though carrying presents, the American delegation met with a definite feeling of *timeo Danaos*.

---

*Nor is this self-denial called for in what concerns Latin America only. The fact is that the vigour of the United States is such that it presses with overwhelming strength on all her neighbours and thus inevitably creates anti-Americanism. This is the case even in Canada. More than one quarter of Canada's industry is controlled by the U.S. Half of Canada's manufacturing and two thirds of her mining, smelting and petroleum interests are owned by U.S. citizens or corporations; and so forth. See "Anti-Americanism grows in Canada", by Arnold Beichmann, in the *New Leader*, 20th November, 1961.

2.—A CHANGE OF HEART

The advent of a new administration, endowed with courage and imagination, affords an excellent opportunity for tackling this most difficult and delicate part of the problem. The way, however, has to be mapped carefully. Paradoxical as it may sound, the danger now may come from the eagerness to do too much too quickly; and the error may well be too much faith in mere action. Not what we do but what we are is what matters.

Let us think less of our programme than of the spirit in which we are going to lay it out. What is wanted is a radical alteration of the way in which the United States, government, public opinion and business community, have stood for generations towards the Latin American world. F. D. Roosevelt's good-neighbour policy was not good enough in this respect, important and generous as the step then was.* Something more thorough is wanted which we, all of us, must endeavour to define.

Here is a contribution to such a definition. First and foremost, the all too frequent attitude of *all-round* superiority towards Latin America should give way to a better realization of the relativity of such relationships, based on a more lively appreciation of the value of variety in human culture. This would entail giving up the conscious or subconscious tendency to equate progress in Latin America with development along lines closer and closer to those of the United States. What is wanted is a sincere appreciation of the value of Latin American culture as it is, and a desire and effort to co-operate in its development as it is.

From this primordial change of heart one might hope other developments would flow. For instance, the almost universal idea prevailing in business—and, what is worse, often also in diplomatic circles—that Latin America is a fair field for all kinds of financial and economic hunting, might be given a well deserved rest. The huge dimensions of modern industry no longer allow the easy-going indifference of nineteeth-century liberalism to rule our behaviour. One may remain faithful to the

* "We are the *good* and they are the *neighbour*" was the current quip in Mexico at the time.

principle of market economy without admitting as a fair application of that theory the unequal struggle between a David nation
and a Goliath industry. Furthermore, world affairs have reached
such a state of solidarity that we no longer think it in the
interests of the United States that a small, ill-organized nation
should be impoverished in order to increase the dividends of a
couple of thousand Americans.

This change of heart, therefore, should lead to a clear perspective of what we want. We want a Latin American continent
healthy in mind and body, free and peaceful. And the ways
thereto may vary but must in fact lead thereto.

3. — LESS SHOW — MORE INTIMACY

We might end here; for if the change of heart is real and
true, every action that follows will be right since it will depend
only on the intellect, and there is no lack of intellect about in the
U.S.A. But stay: how about manner, style and taste? Yes, that
is a question, and by no means unimportant. There is, for instance, propaganda. May I risk the opinion that most propaganda does more harm than good? Information, yes. Propaganda, no. And so, it might be necessary to adopt a less
showy, splashy, sensational style. One ounce of achievement is
worth a ton of advertisement. In fact, a certain casual neglect
of publicity, provided the action concerned were strikingly good,
might do wonders. People are tired of "the most", "the
biggest" and "the best". A hint of surprise at other people's
surprise would considerably enhance the value of what had been
done.

For instance, relations between the United States and the
Latin American nations are perhaps too exclusively formal. The
question of what to do with the OAS must be left for a later
page but a caveat must be entered here about its cold, official
atmosphere. What is wanted is a more informal and frequent
intimacy between leaders of U.S. policy and men widely
respected from Rio Grande to Patagonia, men who are available, free from official responsibilities, rich in experience and

wisdom. A new style, less tense with crises, less loaded with statements and declarations, quieter, simpler, closer to the facts, would do much to clear the air of that distrust and that almost despairing scepticism which now obscure it; and it would initiate a much needed recovery of the moral authority of the United States.

4. — A NEW MANNER FOR U.S. DIPLOMATS

A radical change might be brought about in the manner, style and attitude of the diplomatic representatives of the United States. In a speech delivered in Matamoros (29th November, 1915) President Carranza of Mexico described, in a negative way, what this diplomacy was then and has too often been in recent times:

The leading ideas in international policy are few, clear and simple. They come down to declaring that all countries are equal and must mutually and scrupulously respect their institutions, their laws and their sovereignties; that no country should in any form or for any motive meddle in the internal affairs of other countries; that no man should claim a better condition than that of the citizens of the country where he goes to settle nor turn his status as a stranger into a title for exacting protection and privilege. From this system of principles, a profound change in the present way of understanding diplomacy will flow. It should not be used in order to protect private interests or to put at their service the force and majesty of the nations. Nor should it be made use of in order to exert pressure on the governments of weak countries so as to obtain alteration in their laws when these laws do not suit the interests of the subjects of powerful countries.

The reader of the pages that precede will be aware of the fact that these remarks of the famous Mexican President were by no means mere pious wishes, and that in their negative way they faithfully reflected an all too real state of affairs. A change in the attitude of American diplomacy on the lines suggested by Carranza's speech would soon be felt to the immediate benefit of the moral authority of the United States.

5. — THE UNITED STATES' WAY WITH DICTATORS

Let us be frank and plain about it. Nothing whatever can save the "figure" the United States cuts in Latin America unless her attitude to the still remaining dictatorships is seen to change in fact as well as in words. The U.S. must cut loose from the remaining dictators not only because it is good policy but (to borrow President Kennedy's words) because it is right.

A country, great or small, is not a schoolboy to whom one dictates a programme. The how and the when of the United States' liberation from that moral cannon ball she has dragged for years chained to her foot must be left for the men at the helm to decide. The fact remains that while nothing is done the mistrust of the United States in the whole Hispanic world will remain incurable. An early indication of a change of wind in this matter is an indispensable condition, preliminary to any action; for such action, no matter how well meant, would otherwise be tainted with the continued ambiguity of the new administration as to the basic issue of freedom. A public statement revealing in unmistakable terms the FBI's findings on Dr Galindez's murder might be a good beginning. Other steps would have to follow.

No general declaration of principle would suffice here. The world has heard so many words misfitting so many deeds, has seen so many deeds belying so many words, that what is wanted now is stark, uncommented action. Short of such action, it is hard to see how the moral authority of the U.S. could be revived.

6. — AN OBJECTIVE ENQUIRY

There are, of course, a number of courses of action which would meet Latin American needs and at the same time enhance the name of the United States in the continent. They will be found along the path of sincerity, integrity and what might be described as internal sovereignty, i.e., the ability to set the interests of the U.S. nation and state above those of this or that American individual or corporation.

An example might be useful, but only as such, since other courses of action are open. More than once in the preceding pages the subject of unsatisfactory practices in the financial relations between the two Americas has come to the fore. It is safe to suggest that a thorough enquiry on this delicate question would contribute to improve matters, by a better knowledge of the subject and, if the enquiry were adequately organized, by the way in which it would be carried out.

I have in mind an international but not an inter-statal enquiry; and, though merely as a blueprint subject to discussion and amendment, I may perhaps be rash enough to put forward a plan for its organization and even a list of names. A central invariable core might be set up, composed of such men as Raul Prebisch (who should be chairman), together with a prominent U.S. economist whom I prefer not to designate, and Professor François Perroux of Paris, Lord Robbins of London, Professor W. Röpke of Geneva, Professor Gunnar Myrdal of Stockholm and Signor G. Malagodi of Rome. These men would study the financial and economic relations between the capital-providing countries and Latin America from the Second World War to this day and outline a programme for the future. For the study of any one particular nation, they would co-opt an economist of the nationality concerned.

Need I say that the names suggested are not essential for the success of the idea? I will, nevertheless, point out that their weight is such as to bestow an unrivalled authority upon it. We should then have before the forum of the world an authoritative statement of the position, an objective criticism of the past and a scientific plan of action for the future. But we should gain something more precious still: a tangible witness that the U.S. meant what she said.

There are a number of vexed questions of an economic and

financial nature which might with advantage be referred to this kind of Commission. One of them is that of raw materials and their price, on which, in the view of many Latin Americans, is based one of the systems whereby the continent is being drained of its wealth for the benefit of the rich countries, thus making the rich richer and the poor poorer. Another is that of the supply of capital and experts without political "strings". A third is the situation created by the rapid increase in population and the slow increase in productivity. In general the more thoroughgoing and concrete the enquiry, the greater its technical utility and its moral effect would be.

7.—THROW OFF THE MASK OF MAKE-BELIEVE

The OAS should be thoroughly recast. There is a fundamental make-believe in it, in that it is supposed to be a meeting of equal partners on equal terms, while in fact the U.S.A. dominates the whole. The U.S. would gain much moral power if she insisted on the need to rebuild the whole structure so that it is composed of only two partners: the U.S.A. and Latin America. If this aim were found too ambitious, a middle phase might be attempted. For instance, the OAS might be reduced to five partners: the U.S.A., Brazil; Northern Latin America; South-Western Latin America (from Venezuela to Chile); and South-Eastern Latin America (Argentina, Uruguay, Paraguay and Bolivia). Other groupings might be considered.

These steps towards a federation would not be easy, but the initial impulse would be less difficult than it seems; for the change would not as yet imply any federation of the Latin American States, desirable as such a step would be; it would merely aim at the creation of regional branches of the OAS along the lines suggested.

The U.S.A. has an unimpeachable record with regard to these matters in what concerns Europe. The advantages of wider groupings are no less weighty for the American than they are for the European continent. While Latin America remains dispersed as a dust of weak nations, none of which can compare even in mere order of magnitude with the United States, the OAS can hardly claim to be more than a decorous shield to veil the supremacy of the one over the many without altogether hiding it. This fact confers on everything that happens behind the shield an inevitable insincerity. It leads to and, at times, justifies accusations levelled against the U.S.A. that it is using the organization for carrying out policies wished or designed by the State Department.

8. — LATIN AMERICA'S OWN INSTITUTIONS

It so happens that groupings are already beginning to coalesce in Latin America. No special stress need be laid on the organization of Central American States, which suffers from the tensions prevailing in the area owing to the struggle between democratically run and dictatorially held countries. An ambitious treaty was signed on 8th January, 1959, between Costa Rica, El Salvador, Guatemala, Honduras and Nicaragua establishing a common market. Its chances of survival depend on the future general stability of the zone, but it is a symbol and a symptom of the way things are going.

A weightier event pointing in the same direction is the common market established in virtue of the Treaty of Montevideo (18th February, 1960) between Argentina, Brazil, Chile, Mexico, Paraguay, Uruguay and Peru. This is not the place to analyse it in detail. The fact is noted as an important step towards the political federation of all Latin America which would contribute perhaps more than any other measure or event towards the stabilization of public life on the continent.

It stands to reason that such an evolution would be considerably advanced if the United States were to put her incomparable energies at its service. A number of moves could be made at once, not necessarily within a strictly political framework, but yet of an essentially political nature. They would require Latin American initiative and U.S. encouragement and possibly backing. This encouragement and this backing might in the circumstances be considered almost quixotic. Two or three of such moves might be suggested for discussion.

More than once in the preceding chapters the scarcity of Latin American technicians has been observed. It seems possible nowadays to attempt the establishment of a great technical school on the lines of the Zürich Polytechnicum or of the Boston M.I.T. to meet the needs of the whole of Latin America. It should be financed by the twenty nations. This institution would bind them to some concrete form of co-operation outside mere politics and would encourage the youth of the nations concerned to devote themselves to technical professions. The U.S.A. might help with advice, staff and perhaps some measure of initial financial backing, though this might not be needed.

A federation, possibly a fusion, of all Latin American airlines might be attempted. This would avoid much overlapping and unnecessary expense, and would create another field for co-operation. This federation might be extended to the sea-lines. A sea and air combine of transport for the whole of South America would result, with considerable advantages for the future political federation of the whole continent. It might be extended to include the Post, by creating a Latin American Postal Union.

A kind of prefiguration of a Federal Reserve Bank should be set up, to deal with loans for creative purposes and advice on such matters as inflation, development and increase of production. Economists tell us that Latin America, which counts today 200 million people, is to have 300 million within fifteen years, on the basis of the highest increase in the world (2 to 3 % per year) and that its production increases only by a little over 1 %; they add that the continent will need 35 million new jobs within these fifteen years. It seems the courageous and imaginative thing to do to entrust this formidable work to a Latin American institution. Needless to say, it would have to be started with world capital and to rely on selected experts from the whole free world. But what a relief for all concerned if the work had not to be done under the sole responsibility of the U.S.A. more or less camouflaged with international bunting.

There is yet another institution which might be encouraged, one for which the help of the U.S.A. might exact on her part the greatest abnegation of all: a really Latin American, truly independent press agency. The choice at present is either an American agency such as the UP and AP, or the communist-controlled Cuban agency, *Prensa Latina,* or one or other of the big European agencies. Paradoxical as it may seem at first, the setting up of a truly Latin American press agency controlled by a federation of Latin American newspapers,* excluding fascist and communist organs, would be highly beneficial for the true interests of the United States. Items of news favourable to the U.S.A. would be believed under the imprint of a really free Latin American agency more readily than they are nowadays under that of well-known American sources.

This list of suggestions is by no means exclusive. It is put forward in the belief that, since a coming together of the twenty nations is vital, and since innate and historical tendencies still work for separatism, a number of institutions need not wait for a better political climate, and might be launched in the near future. In their turn, they would pave the way for that better conjuncture which would allow a political federation to emerge.

9. — AGRARIAN REFORM

Short of the recovery of the moral authority of the United States, no event is more urgent for saving Latin America than a thoroughgoing agrarian reform. Here again, urgency should not mean haste. Adequate institutions should be organized, well provided with technicians and funds. Only too often endeavours of this kind fail because of an inadequate knowledge of the medium on the part of the experts sent. The experts may know all that is needed of agriculture and so forth but next to nothing of the people and their ways. This living aspect of the technician needs watching. Anthropologists might with advantage be

---

*Provided these newspapers themselves were not controlled by U.S. capital!

associated with land economists.* The golden rule should be not to generalize, but to try to solve local problems in a local way. The study of the general problem would have be entrusted to a Latin American institution of Agrarian Reform, which would prepare and negotiate the national laws to be voted by Parliaments and the national institutions to be established. This is a much needed and urgent reform to be undertaken without prejudices either for or against this or that form of landowner-ship, but led only by the need to increase production and to better the standard of living and the freedom of the peasant and farmer.

10.—POLITICAL ADVANCEMENT

There would be room also for a scientific centre of political studies covering the whole of Latin America. It would collect the facts, analyse them, suggest solutions and remedies, and stand before public opinion as a detached independent and authoritative observer. For instance, such an institution might well illustrate the need for independent institutions of account-ancy which would stand watch over public and semi-public finances, report on their administration and so prevent the scandalous corruption which has enabled dictators and even democratic presidents to enrich themselves at the expense of their countrymen.

This Institute would be able to perform inestimable services for the prevention of dictatorship and *caudillismo*. A series of scientific monographs, backed by solid information on anthrop-ological conditions, would exert an incalculable influence on public opinion and possibly contribute more than any direct political intervention to eradicate this cancer from Latin Ameri-can and even from Spanish political life.

This is only an example of what such an institution might do. A close watch on political life at all the levels, national,

*Much can be learnt in this respect from two or three of the excellent essays of the treatise often quoted in these pages: *Social Change in Latin America Today.*

provincial, municipal, might enable it to criticize ways and practices and to suggest alterations with an unrivalled authority.
Indirectly, it would contribute to create that higher federal
awareness which must precede any successful attempt at
political federation.

11. — THE PANAMA CANAL

The United States should bear in mind that the Panama
Canal was born in circumstances of open cynical imperialism.
Theodore Roosevelt made no bones about it. "I took Panama."
The time seems ripe for a re-examination of the problem in the
light of:

—the new (hot) war strategies;

—the new balance between hot war and cold war, force and
public opinion. It is now arguable whether the U.S. gains
more in force than she loses in public opinion by retaining that
ill-begotten spot. Senator George D. Aiken, in a report to the
U.S.A. Senate (1960), has proposed an internationalization of
the Canal under the United Nations. With all respect, this
seems to me to sin by too much optimism as to the advantages
of bringing in the Soviet Union with a cargo of vetoes so close
to so narrow a passage. Another solution might be considered:
to place the Canal under a special international body in which
NATO and OAS would be represented. Such a move by the
U.S.A. would powerfully contribute to popularize the U.S.A.
in Latin America.

12. — PUERTO RICO

This island is again another oddity in the Latin American
world. It remained politically dependent on the U.S.A. after
Cuba gained her (political) independence from Spain. It has
so far been well and peacefully governed, so that it has become
in a way a model for the whole Latin American world.

On the other side of the ledger, a number of items can be
noted. The island never was turbulent. It was peaceful while

Cuba fought, and the U.S. just took it from a vanquished Spain on the basis of the right of the victor. It is most generously subsidized by the United States in a number of indirect ways. It found a wise, liberal, democratic leader in Governor Muñoz Marín. Last, but not least, it evacuates and dumps on to New York a dismal crowd of surplus citizens living at the very lowest level in the whole of the U.S.

The question of Puerto Rico is by no means urgent nor of the very first importance for Latin America, but could not be omitted from this survey. In all that is successful, peaceful and prosperous, Puerto Rico should be a model to be studied by other Latin American nations. The U.S. might however revise certain forms of Americanization which still linger from her "colonial" period in the island, such as, for instance, her insistence on American bishops, meekly accepted by the Vatican. Governor Muñoz Marín should be one of the best advisers and guides of the U.S. in the present Latin American troubles. Finally, as for the future, an association of Puerto Rico with a free, liberal-democratic Cuba and an equally free Dominican Republic ought to be studied. It seems now certain that if, after the Spanish-American War, the U.S.A. had federated Cuba, Puerto Rico and the Dominican Republic, the State Department might have spared itself many a headache.

13. — WIDEN THE ALTERNATIVE

One of the natural results of the U.S.A.-centred viewpoint from which Latin American affairs have been considered is that when an antidote is sought for a Soviet action, nothing comes to mind but an U.S.A. anti-action of a similar nature. The Soviet book or pamphlet is countered by an American book or pamphlet, the Soviet expert, by an American expert; the trip to Moscow or to Peking, by a trip to New York or to Boston; studies in a Soviet university by studies in American universities.

Is this enough? Probably not. The United States is by no means lacking in appeal for Latin American youth; but the field is too narrow, the cultural distance not sufficient, the colour and variety not alluring enough to balance what Moscow and Peking have to offer. The time has come for some widening of the effort in every one of those fields. Europe is a rich reservoir of values which young Latin Americans would be keen to tap if adequately helped. Would it be possible for the Atlantic Community to set up an Institute of Cultural Exchange with Latin America? For example, familiarity with the Scandinavian countries and their way of life might have a far healthier effect on Latin Americans than familiarity with the working-class way of life in the U.S.A. And if not, at any rate it would enlarge the experience of the Latin American labour leader or student. A like way of thinking might with advantage be applied to the provision of experts. In short it is desirable to widen the alternative, and not to allow the Latin American average worker, scholar or student to think in terms of either the Soviet or the U.S.A.

14. — A CHANGE IN WORLD POLICY

Since we have more than once endeavoured to set our problem within the framework of the general world struggle, it is but natural that we should stress that no local measure, however felicitous, can save the American continent from the danger of communist disintegration if the world policy followed by the West remains as poor in insight and inspiration as it has been these last eight years.

I do not propose to restate here the reasons I have given elsewhere* to back such a pessimistic view on the way East-West policy has been mismanaged by the West. Within the framework of the present essay all that need be said is that it is not reasonable to expect from Uruguay or Cuba a stiffer attitude towards Moscow than from the U.S.A. or Great Britain; and that before going to Mexico and Cuba Mr. Mikoyan had been invited to the United States. Until the West

*The Blowing-up of the Parthenon, Praeger, New York, Pall Mall Press, London, 1960-61.

develops the courage and the wisdom to have a policy of its own instead of a mere reflection of the policy of the Soviet Union, how can Latin American nations solidly back a western policy that does not really exist? The West is still repeating Moscow's meaningless or misleading slogans such as "Disarmament", "Peaceful Coexistence" and "Peace", and accepting to talk on them, instead of insisting on its own concepts and vocabulary. It was not until President Kennedy's inaugural address that the world heard again the word *freedom* brought to the forefront of political action. May this fact be of good augury.

CONCLUSION

O T H E R lines of action could easily be outlined flowing from the fundamental change of heart and mind posited above. It does not seem indispensable to burden this work with their detailed description. The danger has been defined. The way to meet it has been studied with a deep concern for the evil to be prevented, for its causes, and for the higher interests of the United States. If in the process of describing some of the causes of the trouble the reader has felt that a word was too vivacious, a judgment too harsh, no one would regret it more than the author. The aim of this work has been to eliminate a some-what irrelevant obstacle to the right evolution of mankind. This evolution rises from the animal to the spiritual, from force to thought. Nationalism would revert it towards the animal level and would turn nations into herds. Communism would reverse it back not merely to the animal level but to the merely inert, the flat equality of the grains of sand in a desert. Liberal democratic philosophy is therefore the only forward-looking political school of thought there is. For good or ill, the U.S.A. must incarnate this philosophy, and the defence of this way of life against the two dangers that threaten it must become the primordial duty of the nation which was born under the banner of freedom.

INDEX